Dedication

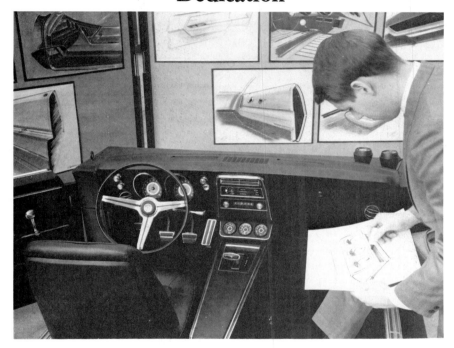

To the men and women of Chevrolet who designed and built it

Michael Antonick

Illustrated
CAMARO
BUYER'S
GUIDE T.M.

Motorbooks International
Publishers & Wholesalers Inc.
Osceola, Wisconsin 54020, USA ®

First published in 1985 by Motorbooks International
Publishers & Wholesalers Inc, PO Box 2, 729 Prospect
Avenue, Osceola, WI 54020 USA

Library of Congress Cataloging-in-Publication Data

Antonick, Mike
    Illustrated Camaro buyer's guide.

    Bibliography: p.
    1. Automobiles—Purchasing.   2. Camaro automobile.
I. Title.   II.Title: Camaro buyer's guide.
TL162.A58   1987   619.2'222   87-12203
ISBN 0-87938-262-7 (soft)

CREDITS AND ACKNOWLEDGEMENTS

Thanks to all who contributed in any way to the information and photos contained in this book. Special mention goes to the following people.

Ed Cunneen, for technical assistance and for photographing his own 1969 Z-28 as the model for the cover illustration.

Carl Dwiggins of Village Motors in Conover, North Carolina, who has more Camaros in his collection than I could count, for permitting me to photograph his cars on very short notice.

Mike Lamm, noted Camaro book author, for permitting me to peruse his extensive Camaro library, and for his expert editing of this book's first draft.

Bob McDorman, for giving me access to his Canal Winchester, Ohio, Chevrolet dealership files and library, and for permitting me to photograph dealership Camaros and Camaros from his personal collection.

Dan Byers for assembling the price survey.

Brian Hardy and John Hepperle for permitting me to photograph their Camaros.

Gary Lisk and Denny Mumaw for help with facts and figures.

Steve Pollock for technical assistance and editing.

Reid Williamson for help with pricing data.

And to everyone at Chevrolet Motor Division.

Finally, to the authors and publishers of the following Camaro books:

The Camaro Book, From A Through Z-28, Michael Lamm/Lamm-Morada Publishing.

Camaro, The Third Generation, Michael Lamm/Lamm-Morada Publishing.

Camaro! From Challenger to Champion, Gary Witzenburg/Princeton Publishing Company.

Camaro 1967-1969 Fact Book, M. F. Dobbins, F. J. R. Incremona/Dr. M. F. Dobbins.

Mike Antonick

TABLE OF CONTENTS

INTRODUCTION

The mere writing of *Illustrated Camaro Buyer's Guide* implies that Camaros have become more than sporty, affordable cars. It implies they've entered the hallowed ground of the car collector; that they've become appreciating investments.

Describing Camaros as sporting cars is one thing, but can calling them collector cars be justified? Can any vehicle whose production totaled a million in its sixth year be thought of in investment terms? Doesn't an automobile have to have some measure of scarcity to be valid collector material?

Not necessarily. Scarcity no more ensures collectibility than a lack of scarcity rules it out. But even if you subscribe to the rarity theory, be advised that some Camaros are plenty rare. There were, for instance, sixty-nine special Camaros built in 1969 with aluminum-block, 427-cubic-inch-displacement engines that just may have been the fastest production automobiles ever sold in this country. Of those sixty-nine ZL-1 models, about half are known to still exist, and just a handful are complete and original. Is that rare enough?

When it made its debut on September 29, 1966—and for several years into production—the Camaro had an option list a mile long; so long, few within GM's innards, let alone its dealers and customers, could decipher it. It is this incredible option menu that has indeed created many Camaros that do meet every collector car criteria. Camaros were designed to fit a specific market segment, yet there were many different kinds of Camaros. Some are extremely rare and almost priceless, some are desirable cars that will hold or increase in value, many others offer little more than other used cars as they all depreciate their way into local auto graveyards.

Clearing away the option fog, learning which Camaros will meet your expectations and goals, and evaluating a Camaro's condition correctly are the keys to making a smart Camaro purchase. But unless you've bought and sold scores of them, or done a mountain of research, you'll need some help. That's what *Illustrated Camaro Buyer's Guide* is for.

In order to understand the reasons behind the emergence of some Camaros as hot speculative investments, it's necessary to review the circumstances that literally forced Chevrolet to develop the car in the first place. Ford's Mustang arrived in April 1964. Had it been only a mild success, odds are there would never have been a Camaro.

But the Mustang wasn't merely a success, it was *wildly* successful beyond anyone's, including Ford's, expectations. Whatever new-car sales records were kept, Mustang broke them.

General Motors had no choice but to respond with a market challenger, and did so by launching a crash program in August 1964. Its response to the Mustang had to come from its Chevrolet Division, which had plenty of car lines to sell in 1964. (Along with the full-size Chevrolet, there were the Chevelle, the Corvette, the Corvair and the one everyone picked as the most unimaginative name ever selected for a Chevrolet product—the Chevy II.) General Motors uses letters to designate car lines internally, and the Camaro became the F-car. During early development, the nameplate mentioned as most likely to be used was Panther.

By the time the Camaro was ready, GM had lost two and a half years in sales to the Mustang, some 1.3 million cars. To put it mildly, GM missed the marketing boat on this one. Yet it isn't entirely fair to give all the credit to Ford for launching the ponycar phenomenon. The signals were there for all to see. General Motors simply missed them; Ford, specifically Lee Iacocca, didn't.

Ironically, GM itself generated signals that should have led it to the Camaro sooner. Its own Corvair, the most radical of the Big Three's 1960 entries into the compact market, was something of a dud until the Corvair Monza series came along with bucket seats and other sporty accouterments, and sold much better. The car wasn't much different, but customers responded to the image switch.

Similarly, Pontiac's GTO was a slick transformation of a pleasant little family sedan into a street-scorching musclecar by little more than the addition of power and sporty (there's that word again) trim. Talk about image! Listen to what Pontiac said in its 1964 GTO dealer brochure: "To be perfectly honest, the GTO is not everyone's cup of tea. Designed as a piece of performance machinery, its purpose in life is to permit you to make the most of your driving skill. Its suspension is firm, tuned more to the open road than to wafting gently over bumpy city streets. Its dual exhausts won't win any prizes for whispering. And, unless you order it with our lazy 3.08:1 low-ratio rear axle, its gas mileage won't be anything to write home about." Pretty racy prose from the stodgy old General, and quite a contrast to today's "your mileage may vary. . . ."

Both the Corvair Monza and GTO success stories were signals of a market potential that somehow escaped the decisionmakers at General Motors. The Corvair was the heart of GM's dilemma. Even when the Mustang entered the marketplace, many within GM still scoffed at what they figured was a low-budget attempt to put a sporty body on the Falcon and pass it off as a new sports car. Those who adhered to this thinking assumed the public wouldn't fall for this phony pony. Even when initial Mustang sales were strong, they thought, the beautifully restyled 1965 Corvair, due for release just five months after the first Mustang, would plow Ford's entry under for good.

The public's view was different. It saw the Mustang as the all-new car. So what if it shared some mechanical components with the Falcon? Didn't all cars do that sort of thing? The Mustang name was new. Its introduction came at a different time of year. Most Mustangs had bucket seats, and none had four doors. In bare-bones attire, the Mustang was inexpensive, but a luxury car or a hot performer, or both, could be ordered to suit. For most people, just the appearance of sportiness was enough. Ford's interpretation of a new American sports car was right on the mark.

By contrast, the public wasn't sure what GM was up to with the Corvair. There were sporty jobs with turbocharging on the one hand, and dour-looking four-door sedans with funny little dash-mounted Powerglide shift levers on the other.

Plus, Corvairs had real problems. Dirt-simple Falcons and Valiants were logging troublefree miles for their conservative owners, but Corvairs were developing nasty traits. The Corvair's mechanical novelty was backfiring. Its rear-mounted aluminum engine turned out to be a notorious oil-leaker. Since it was air-cooled, there was no hot water to circulate through a heater core; for cabin heat, air was pulled across the engine's hot exhaust manifolds. If the exhaust manifolds leaked, raw exhaust fumes were pulled into the heating system. At best, the oily engine would engulf occupants desiring warmth with the scent of smoldering Quaker State.

The Corvair's major drawback was its lack of adaptability. Ford could build the Mustang with a six-cylinder engine and automatic transmission for the customers who wanted reliable, inexpensive transportation with a little flair. The Mustang would also accept potent V-8 engines and encroach conveniently into the GTO's musclecar market. By contrast, the Corvair was designed around its flat, six-cylinder engine in back. There were real limits both on that engine's enlargement potential and on the car's inherent ability to handle more power if something else were wedged in.

Ralph Nader's attack on the Corvair came during 1964, but *after* GM gave the green light for the Camaro's development program. Nader was a public relations disaster for GM and the Corvair, and ultimately the whole mess sealed the Corvair's fate. Give him credit for that, but not for prompting GM to build the Camaro. It was the Mustang's displacement flexibility and the Corvair's lack of it that made the difference.

Since we're handing out credit, Chevrolet deserves much for its approach to the Camaro. It should have been first in the marketplace with a Camaro-like vehicle, and it was slow to respond to the writing on the wall when the Mustang scored an immediate home run. But once the green light came on, Chevrolet responded as only a division of mighty General Motors can.

It was too late to be first, so Chevrolet decreed its Camaro had to be better. Ford fans would argue the point, and it took the Camaro until 1977 to overtake the Mustang in annual sales, but Chevrolet pulled out the big guns for its Mustang-assault vehicle. Details will follow in the model-by-model chapter rundowns, so just understand for now that these Chevrolet people took the challenge very seriously. The embarrassment inflicted by Ford is one reason the Camaro came out so well. That's not to say Camaros don't have faults; from the earliest models to the present, they do. The car has always had to be affordable, meaning corners got cut. But in terms of who could design and build the best car for the market segment being contested, the Chevrolet people were determined to set the record straight.

This "Let's go get 'em" attitude resulted in a very good Camaro at introduction, and an even better one as bugs were ironed out and new features added. Right from the start, the Camaro was an excellent value. Sales have had their ups and downs, but the Camaro has continued to offer a lot of automobile for the money against the competition. Now, hindsight is telling many enthusiasts that Chevrolet has built some Camaros during the past two decades that make excellent choices as collector cars, or even everyday cars that will hold or appreciate in value.

One reason is what has happened to the marketplace in general. The first Camaros came along right on the heels of federal government influence on auto production with safety and emission mandates. But the effects on the first Camaro generation, the 1967-69 models, were minimal. As federal requirements tightened each year, both weight increases and power reductions afflicted almost every new automobile sold in the United States. In 1974, Chevrolet seriously considered dumping the Camaro, thinking it was being mandated away from its intended mission, something declining sales seemed to validate. But Chevrolet hung on, because too many people inside Chevrolet thought the Camaro was too good to lose. They were right. Sales of the second-generation Camaro, introduced as a late-1970 model, eventually recovered and flourished after 1976. The beautiful new Camaros we see today are the third generation, which started as the 1982 model.

Illustrated Camaro Buyer's Guide divides Camaros into three generations and then groups one or more models into each chapter. As an overview, let's take a brief look at each Camaro generation.

The first-generation Camaros are the 1967-69 models. These "early" Camaros are creating the most enthusiast interest today. They were the least touched by government regulation, and the long list of optional engines made possible some blisteringly fast automobiles. These Camaros were direct Mustang competitors and properly belong in the ponycar category, but big-engine Camaros also catch the eye of musclecar enthusiasts, no small group these days. All first-generation Camaros were two-doors, available in both coupe and convertible body styles.

First-generation Camaros were excellent automobiles for their day. Power output, even from the smaller engines, was smooth and strong. Features like air conditioning, power windows, cruise control and tilt steering wheel were Camaro options throughout the first generation.

But if evaluated from an everyday driving standpoint, first-generation Camaros aren't in the same league as newer Camaros. The early Camaros ride somewhat harshly, compounded by flat, short, relatively unadjustable seats. So you'll pay more for less when measuring ride and comfort quality. However, many first-generation Camaros are unquestionably appreciating the fastest, so they're excellent investments.

General Motors entered the ponycar market with a Camaro aimed squarely at the Mustang, so compromises were made in the first-generation cars to keep them cost competitive. Though the Camaro was generally well received by the motoring press, some writers criticized the more glaring compromises, such as single-leaf rear springs that had hopping tendencies when power was applied, also slow steering, smallish drum brakes (the disc option was fine) and cowl shake. Much was corrected by the end of the first generation, but Chevrolet had the chance to do a "clean-sheet" Camaro for 1970. It resulted in one of America's all-time great automobiles. The late-introduction 1970 Camaro, often referred to as the 1970½, was a gorgeous styling exercise that drew praise both in America and abroad.

The beauty of the second generation was more than skin deep. Below the beautiful exterior was a new chassis, similar in concept to the first generation, but with all the necessary refinements to make the Camaro a real world-class car. Facelifted twice, the second-generation Camaro design was good enough to last through 1981. Not many cars can make that claim, especially since the decade of the seventies was a most turbulent one for automobiles. Government mandates jelled, and high-compression engines were detuned or phased out. Two gasoline supply crises spelled the end of many fuel-inefficient cars. The Camaro wasn't a guzzler, but neither has it ever been an economy special. Yet, the second-generation Camaro lived through it all.

Second-generation Camaros with high-compression engines are already recognized as very desirable cars, and more are being added to the list. At the least, many Camaros built during the seventies should offer the opportunity to drive great-handling, sporty cars at little or no depreciation. But beware: Buried among the gems are many Camaros with little to distinguish themselves.

The inherent value of second-generation Camaros hasn't escaped the experts.

In 1971, *Road & Track* magazine picked the Camaro as one of the world's ten best cars. It was the only American car in the group. In its July 1983 issue, *Road & Track* presented its pick of the ten best used enthusiast cars for under $5,000. The second-generation Camaro made the list (*Road & Track* especially liked the 1970-73 models), and it was again the only American car on the list. *Road & Track* called the Camaro the best-looking American car of the seventies, and among the best of any decade. Find one well-cared-for and rust free, said *Road & Track,* and you could pretty much forget abou. mechanical problems, because the Camaro had an excellent reliability record.

The accolades given the third Camaro generation, which started with the 1982 model, are so common and fresh in memory they hardly need review. They range from *Car and Driver's* selection of the 1984 Camaro as the best-handling car built in America, to *Road & Track's* choice (May 1984) of the Camaro as one of the world's twelve best cars. Third-generation Camaros aren't old enough to be talked about in the same collector-investment lingo as the older models, but they will be eventually. For now, they are simply among the best in new- and used-car values.

Significantly, the third generation confirms just how right the Camaros before it were. Against all predictions of a shrunk-down, front-wheel-drive, four- or six-cylinder car, Chevrolet started with a clean sheet, looked at the facts, then designed a brand-new Camaro that was remarkably similar in size, layout and construction to its very first Mustang challenger of 1967.

There is a common thread running through all Camaro generations, called the Z-28. The Z first materialized in 1967 as a road racer to compete with the Mustang in the Trans-Am series. General Motors wasn't officially involved in racing, of course; it just happened to offer a production car that could do the job nicely, thank you. The increasing federal safety and emission requirements took a particular toll on the Z-28; in 1975, Chevrolet decided to drop it rather than just hang Z-28 nameplates on a Camaro that wasn't up to snuff. But it came back in mid-1977 with the emphasis on handling. In time, much of the lost power came back, too. Because of the Z-28's dominance of the Camaro's entire history, it's often assumed that if a Camaro isn't a Z-28, it isn't worth an enthusiast's consideration. Not true. There's no question about the Z-28's status, and many Z-28's are tremendous collector cars. But there are others, as we shall see.

In the year that I gathered information for this book, I visited Chevrolet at the GM Tech Center in Warren, Michigan, several times, and also traveled to California to talk with Michael Lamm, the Camaro book author. I read what Mike and others have written about the Camaro. I amassed a considerable Camaro library consisting of owners manuals, dealership literature, every Chevrolet dealership price and option guide (as many as seven in a single model year) and over 1,000 photos, some from Chevrolet, some my own. I went through every *Road & Track* published since 1965 to see how it had perceived the Camaro at the time, and I compared the editors' comments to those of other magazines. I looked into the current marketplace, requesting catalogs from every Camaro aftermarket supplier I could locate. And I talked to other Camaro enthusiasts, owners, restorers and buffs to get as wide a perspective as possible.

Through all this, I was surprised to find myself most often comparing the Camaro not to the Mustang, but to the Corvette. The Camaro and Corvette are the two genuine enthusiast cars offered by Chevrolet. Excluding the Firebird, Pontiac's sporty car that has always shared many components with the Camaro, the Corvette and Camaro were the only real enthusiast cars offered by General Motors until the Fiero came along for 1984. For two decades, Camaros and Corvettes have shared Chevrolet showrooms. Some customers drawn in by the Corvette settled on the Camaro for its lower cost, extra seats, lower insurance or general utility advantages. Corvette owners whose families grew moved over to the Camaro. And more components than I'd at first realized, especially in the engine bay, have been shared by the two.

Having written a number of Corvette books, I'm quite familiar with Chevrolet's two-seater. Whenever I looked into some facet of the Camaro market, there was a tendency to compare it to the equivalent in the Corvette's. For example, if I were evaluating a Corvette for purchase, and it had worn seats or bad inner door panels, I would know if those components were available as quality reproductions and I would also know their cost. But the Camaro aftermarket, while getting better every day, isn't nearly so far along as the Corvette's. Some things are available, many aren't.

There are some obvious reasons. The different trim levels, color combinations and overall option load for Camaros mean that a wide range of reproductions is necessary. But the cost to do quality reproductions is high. Corvette customers have been willing to pay a high price because the value of a restored Corvette is relatively high. Before Camaro prices started to climb recently, the market values just didn't justify the costs to tool up many reproduction parts.

The Camaro market itself is much more diverse than the Corvette's. Corvettes have at times had lots of options available, too, but the market segment Corvettes appeal to is rather tight. The Camaro appeals to a much broader range of buyers. The majority of Camaro owners are not in the car enthusiast category per se, and don't seek out reproduction or NOS (new old stock) parts to keep their Camaros factory-original. There are Camaro clubs and Camaro shows, but not nearly so many as for the Corvette. A fair percentage of Corvette drivers still wave to each other. Wave to another Camaro, and you'll get a blank stare in return.

Illustrated Camaro Buyer's Guide isn't aimed at the entire Camaro ownership population. It's aimed at the Camaro enthusiast, and especially at the potential Camaro enthusiast. Even though Camaro production has exceeded the Corvette's by tenfold in some years, when the real enthusiasts are boiled out, there are probably similar numbers in each camp.

Because of the quantity difference, finding just any Camaro is easier than finding just any Corvette. But because the Corvette hobby offers so many sources of top-condition cars (shows, clubs, monthly magazines), finding a great Camaro is more difficult than finding a great Corvette.

This is good and bad. Bad because there's a lot of Camaro junk to wade through. Bad because the complexity of options and lack of precise value guidelines confuse a lot of buyers. Good because there are still Camaro bargains out there. There are Camaro owners who don't realize their cars have appreciated significantly. Let's face it, we all love a deal.

But don't be too greedy. There's a story that surfaces every spring about an ad in someone's local newspaper for a $300 1953 Chevy that turns out to be a 1953 Corvette worth 100 times that. The seller is usually an elderly lady whose husband has met his demise in the French Foreign Legion or such. Sometimes it's a 1957 fuel-injected Corvette, and the seller is an unknowing attorney cleaning up an estate. In the introduction to his excellent *Illustrated Porsche Buyer's Guide,* Dean Batchelor tells of a similar tale that circulates among Porsche nuts, something about a disgruntled lady who advertises her ex-husband's pristine 911SC for $100 because he told her to sell it and send him half the proceeds.

Because great Camaros coincided with U.S. involvement in Vietnam, stories about 1969 Z-28's with 300 miles purchased for peanuts usually have the "He went to Nam and didn't come back" line in them somewhere. Sadly, I'm sure some young men did leave their Camaros behind, but you'd be advised not to look for such a situation today.

But as much as any car I know of, Camaros do offer chances to make some really excellent purchases. It's such a complex market, though, that few have a handle on it. How much longer this will last, no one can say. Still, don't rush into anything; better to pass on a good buy than jump at a bad one. One of the Camaro's drawbacks, the quantity built, is also an advantage: If you miss one, there'll likely be another.

How do you locate your dream Camaro? If you desire a fairly new one, all the normal channels, like newspapers and Chevrolet dealers, will do fine. If you wish something more special, you'll need to expand your search. Specialty auto magazines with cars for sale, like *Hemming's Motor News* and *Cars & Parts,* are good sources. Check to see if there's a club in your area. If so, join or at least attend one meeting and let them know what you're after.

Talk to the folks at your local Chevy dealership. Have the salespeople keep their eyes open for a Camaro trade-in. You'll pay a dealer more for a newer Camaro than it would cost from a private individual, but that's not necessarily true for older models. Let the guys in the parts department know what you're looking for. Maybe they'll let you put up a sign on the bulletin board. Every owner of an older Camaro winds up back at the dealer's parts counter from time to time.

It's important to spread yourself around. As with most cars, the good ones are often sold by word of mouth. To have the word passed to you, you need to get the word out. Don't pass up the chance to investigate an available Camaro that isn't exactly what you're after—Camaros attract Camaros. The seller might have more than one, or may know where there's another. If you know of a fabulous Camaro not for sale, let the owner know you'd be interested if the car is ever available. And keep in touch—eventually, everything's for sale.

Locating potential Camaros to purchase isn't as difficult or important as the scrutiny you must give the candidates. It used to be that used Camaros weren't worth enough to justify any great expense in making them look better than they were. Now the situation has changed, and you can't assume a pretty-looking Camaro is pretty all the way through.

Watch for wrecks and rust. The reason these two factors are so important lies in the ways Camaros were constructed. There are two basic ways to build cars: First is the classic body-and-frame construction. This is just what it sounds like; there's a frame with chassis components bolted to it, and a separate body which bolts to the frame. This is great for restoration. You can practically disassemble this sort of construction back to the elements the factory started with and rebuild the car from scratch. The frame can be acid-dipped or sand-blasted, straightened and repaired as needed. (The Corvette is a prime example of body/frame construction, and the fiberglass body never rusts. Corvette frames do rust and sometimes have to be replaced. It's expensive, but it can be and is being done because a Corvette's value can justify it.)

The other way to manufacture cars is called unitized construction. In this case, the frame is eliminated. The body structure is beefed-up as needed, and the chassis components bolt directly to it. Unitized construction generally means fewer materials are needed. That means lower manufacturing costs. A unitized car should also be lighter, which means better fuel economy. So far the unitized construction sounds pretty good, right?

There are problems. Unitized construction requires some slick engineering to give the body the right stiffness and flexing characteristics. And it's tougher to isolate road noise and vibration in a unitized car.

For the restorer, unitized construction can be a nightmare. Some chassis components can be unbolted, but the body itself is a welded-together unit. Anyone looking at a unitized-body car as an investment must obviously place great emphasis on locating something that hasn't been twisted in a wreck, or had structural rust.

First- and second-generation Camaros were built as compromises between body/frame and unitized construction. A fully unitized body was considered for its cost advantages, but the ride and noise isolation of body/frame construction were important, too. So Camaro engineers gave the Camaro a frame up front where it matters most, then used unitized construction for the rear. This continued through the 1981 model. Computer analysis techniques had progressed so far by the late seventies that the third-generation Camaro was fully unitized, although it did get one major bolt-on front cross-member.

First- and second-generation Camaros aren't as bad as fully unitized cars from the restoration angle, but they're not as good as full body/frames either. The bottom line is not to buy a wreck or rust bucket. I realize that anything is fixable if you're willing to throw enough money at it, and maybe this is the sort of resurrection you enjoy. But with just a few exceptions, Camaros don't justify the cost of *properly* fixing a wreck or rustout. Take my word for it, the dollars just don't work out.

Be suspicious of any Camaro that's spent its life in salt air, or where salt is applied to winter roads, regardless of the stored-in-a-heated-garage claims. And don't assume a Camaro from a "rust-free" area like California, is any guarantee. If you find a Camaro from such an area, be sure it came from there originally. Warm-weather states have historically drawn new residents from colder areas — it might have spent a few winters in Buffalo before moving to Pasadena.

Many states known for warm, dry climates also have mountains and snow. States bordering on the ocean have salty air areas that rot cars thoroughly. Even if all the likely rust conditions are ruled out, rust is still possible. I once bought what I thought was a perfect southern California specimen only to find out later that the doors had rusted from the inside. The metal was thin as tissue paper, literally held together by the exterior paint, which still looked great. Someone had stuffed rags into the bottom of the doors to deaden road noise, and the rags held moisture that slipped by the glass seals during an occasional shower or washing. This sort of rust example is usually localized and fixable. But it's nice to know about it before the deal is set, so the repair cost can be built into the purchase price.

There are some specific areas you should check for rust in Camaros. In first-generation cars, look at the forward surface of the dash, just where it meets the windshield. Condensation can cause this area to rust through. Fixing it isn't a simple matter of unbolting the dash, because the dash is welded into the unitized body assembly. To repair it, you've got to pull the windshield and make localized metal repairs, or cut sections out and reweld them.

Rusting floor pans are common in all Camaros. Look under the carpets for rust that starts from the inside as a result of a poor windshield seal. Look at the floor for rust from underneath as well.

Open the door and check the hems (along the bottom surface where the outer door skin is "hemmed" over the inner door panel). If they're rusty, the doors could be on the verge of rusting through. While you're looking at the hems, check the drain holes in the bottoms of the doors. These are there to drain water that slips by the door glass seals. Don't be too alarmed by a little surface rust around the drain holes because that area often becomes damp. But if the holes are plugged, the lower door areas could be seriously rusted from inside. Pull the inner door trim panels and take a look.

A rear window leak can allow water into the trunk. In Camaros, this water finds its way into the lower rear-quarter area and can start rusting from inside. Just because the trunk itself looks clean, don't assume water hasn't gotten in.

Check around the wheelwells, especially if the Camaro has bright wheelwell trim. As nice as the trim looks, it traps debris that starts rust. Every place where the trim is screwed into the wheel lip is a raw-metal exposure inviting rust.

The front subframes of first- and second-generation Camaros are usually not rust problems. They were made of heavy-gauge metal with box sections, and tended to flush themselves clean. If you find a Camaro with a rotted-out front subframe, chances are the whole car is rusted beyond repair. However, it is possible for some localized rusting to occur in subframes at the body-mount locations, particularly the two toward the front. If this happens, you'll have to weld in a repair section or just replace the subframe. There are hundreds of good subframes in junkyards across the country.

First-generation Camaro convertibles were structurally weak and sometimes tended to sag in the middle. This can happen if the unitized body is weakened by rust or, in a structurally sound car, just by years of use. You can spot a convertible with "the sags" by checking the door gap (the space between the door edge and body). The size of the gap should be about three-sixteenths inch, though that can vary from car to car. What's important is the consistency of the gap. If it's pinched tight at the top near the door handle but open a half inch at the bottom, you've found a sagging convertible.

I'm told that a good frame shop can bend a sagging convertible back into shape for about $500. I've also talked to enthusiasts who've gone through this and now swear they'll never own another Camaro convertible. I don't know about you, but trying to bend a seriously sagging car back into shape doesn't settle too well with me. As of this writing, no particular problems have been reported with the convertible Camaros Chevrolet unveiled in 1987.

I recently sold an automobile to a gentleman who really impressed me as knowing how to scrutinize a potential auto purchase, then how to bargain for the best price. Let me describe how he went about it, because his technique was perfect for Camaros.

First, the potential buyer spent a half hour talking to me on the phone about my car. This was a long-distance call (I'd placed ads in all major city newspapers within a four-hour drive), yet he ran through a thirty-item checklist prepared for him by a friend who owned a car similar to mine and knew its weaknesses. Once he was convinced my car was a serious candidate, he made an appointment to see the car, and he called the night before the appointment to confirm it.

When this gent arrived to look at the car, he came prepared with floor jack,

jack stands, tools, trouble light, another checklist and a serial-number guide. He slipped on a set of coveralls and spent an hour under the car looking, probing and poking. That done, he gave the interior, exterior and trunk and engine compartments a thorough going-over. Next came a half-hour test drive with me as passenger. He didn't abuse the car, but he checked every function. Satisfied so far, he had one last request. He asked me to drive my car while he followed in another. This was so that he could observe my car from the rear to be sure it was tracking properly. I suppose he also looked for wobbling rims, and blue puffs from the exhausts which could indicate worn rings or valve guides.

After the inspection was completed, price negotiations began. The buyer didn't tell me my price was ridiculous. He said it was fair, except for the cost of repairing the things he'd uncovered which should be deducted. I said the asking price already took those things into account. We split the difference.

That's the way to buy a collectible Camaro. Often you'll not get through the sequence because you'll find something to wash the deal out. You'll come across sellers who expect you to buy the car after a five-minute inspection and get irritated if you take longer. Move on. You'll want to buy your Camaro from an owner who's proud of it, pleased to show you everything.

It's not that you're searching for perfection, but you need a thorough inspection to evaluate what the car needs. There's a tendency in all of us, upon finding a car that appears very nice, to try to seal the deal quickly for fear the seller might change his mind, or someone else will walk up and buy the car out from under us. It happens, but in the long run caution wins over impulse.

Should you bring a Camaro "expert" with you to evaluate your potential purchase? It depends how well you've done your homework, and how expert your expert is. Mechanically, Camaros are, and have always been, pretty simple cars. The Camaro's market slot has always required that Chevrolet be cost conscious, so all have had conventional drivelines with front engines, driveshafts and solid rear axles. Fanciers of exotic European machinery might think the Camaro unsophisticated, but simple components sure make buying a used Camaro less risky. A Camaro may not be in the same sophistication league as a Ferrari, where a mistake in evaluating an engine could force you into a second mortgage on the family digs to set it right. I'm not telling you to ignore the mechanical aspects of a potential Camaro purchase, but if you have decent mechanical savvy, you'll be able to estimate those restoration costs with greater accuracy than things more specific to the Camaro, like body and trim components.

If the Camaro you're considering needs restoration—particularly if it needs unique components like seats, carpeting and trim items—you have to be able to estimate replacement costs accurately (assuming replacements are available). If you know someone who's gone through a similar restoration, ask him or her. Whether you know someone or not, build your own library of aftermarket supplier catalogs.

There's a controversy in Camaro-land regarding what constitutes an "original" car. With Corvettes, if a part or option wasn't factory-installed, it's wrong. Period. But during the first several years of Camaro production, Chevrolet made numerous parts (usually high-performance) available as dealer options, or across-the-counter for installation by owners. Consequently, many Camaro enthusiasts find nothing wrong with modifying their cars any way they choose, provided Chevrolet parts are used. In their eyes, these cars are still "original," and they have no qualms about advertising them as such.

Personally, I think the most valuable Camaros are those equipped just as they left the factory gates. I know of Camaro owners who've modified their cars but have kept every receipt and every part removed. That's fine. And there are certain components, like the aluminum crossram intake manifold, that I wouldn't hesitate to put on my '69, provided I kept records of everything. But the idea that an owner can make any change he cares to without devaluing the Camaro just won't wash with serious collectors.

Here's where the quantity of Camaros built comes into focus. The special Camaros are the ones that have been untouched, the ones with documentation like original window stickers, warranty plates, invoices, receipts and other papers. This, plus the desirable models and options, is what separates everyday Camaros from collectible Camaros.

The worst mistake you can make in your Camaro purchase is to try to save a few dollars by selecting a Camaro that requires a lot of work. The less the Camaro needs, the more accurately you'll be able to estimate costs. If the car has more wrong with it than right, I guarantee you'll underestimate refurbishing expense every time. So unless you want an every-nut-and-bolt restoration experience, be willing to pay a little more for a Camaro that needs less.

The following chapters each cover one or more model years. They'll help you narrow your preferences before the actual search begins. If you already have a favorite, I'd suggest you at least read all the chapters for Camaros in the same generation. For instance, if 1969 is your pick, read the 1967 and 1968 chapters, too, because there will be references to the 1969 in them.

One message that comes through in this book is that Camaros are both simple and complex. They've all had two doors, either in coupe, convertible, or hatch configuration. They're all front-engine, rear-drive cars with many off-the-shelf components.

But to keep the Camaro's appeal broad, Chevrolet has made a staggering array of options available for the Camaros over the years. It'll be perplexing at first, but getting a handle on it will enable you to zero-in on a Camaro that suits you perfectly. You'll find it worth the effort.

INVESTMENT RATING

✪✪✪✪✪   These are the proven winners and the best investments. They're already expensive and will continue to appreciate at rates higher than other Camaros. These are special cars, often traded or sold among collectors, occasionally advertised in enthusiast magazines, but never found on used car lots.

✪✪✪✪   These are very good investments. The prices are lower than five-star-rated Camaros, but strong appreciation can still be expected. The best ones are sold among enthusiasts, but all the normal car-buying channels can yield four-star Camaros if you're selective.

✪✪✪   These are less expensive than four- or five-star-rated Camaros, but still offer investment potential. Their price and availability tend to make them attractive to first-time buyers. In time, some three-star Camaros might gain collector interest and evolve into four-star status.

✪✪   These are nice Camaros to drive and enjoy. Some could become investment material in the years to come, but you shouldn't buy one now with value appreciation in mind. They look and act like Camaros, but few people consider them special enough to qualify as collector cars.

✪   These are the rest of 'em. These are the Camaros that have been abused, modified, or badly rusted, had engine transplants, or are just completely undistinguished in their option content.

The star rating system above requires interpretation. The option list for many Camaro models was so long that it isn't possible to build all the variables into any rating system. This book gives an overall rating to each Camaro model or model group, then highlights some obvious exceptions. Use these ratings as base guidelines from which to add or deduct for specific Camaros.

For example, let's say a 1970 model interests you. It has an overall rating of three stars, but this assumes it's a Camaro with equipment and condition to merit collector interest. At least three-fourths of all 1970 Camaros alive today are one-star Camaros, but we don't care about those. The 1970 ratings step up at half-star increments for the SS350, SS396 and Z-28 models. An extra half-star is added if the 1970 has Rally Sport equipment. This means a 1970 Z-28 (four and a half stars) with the Rally Sport option (another half star) is a five-star Camaro investment, right? Maybe. It means a 1970 Z-28 Rally Sport is *potentially* a five-star Camaro investment. It has the credentials, but if it had a shady past, an ugly color combination, an option content that simply didn't fit its personality, or any number of other problems, forget five stars.

Is documentation important? Yes. With few exceptions, no Camaro deserves five-star status without "paperwork" like the original window sticker, sales receipts, or warranty plate. Some collectors I spoke with add at least $1,000 to a Camaro's value if it's well documented. Others suggested deducting a full star for any Camaro without documentation.

Lastly, you shouldn't cross-reference the star ratings in this book to other books in the *Illustrated Buyer's Guide* series. The ratings in this book compare Camaros to Camaros.

<table>
<tr><td rowspan="6">

CHAPTER 1
1967 Camaro

</td><td>★★★</td></tr>
<tr><td>★★★(SS350</td></tr>
<tr><td>★★★★ SS396</td></tr>
<tr><td>★★★★★ Z-28, Pace Car</td></tr>
<tr><td>Add (for Rally Sport</td></tr>
<tr><td>Add (for convertible</td></tr>
</table>

1967 Model Production: 220,906

General Motors was America's largest company when Ford unleashed its Mustang in 1964. Everyone knew it was just a matter of time before GM fought back, and the General made no bones about its intentions.

The idea was to take on the Mustang with a Chevrolet challenger that was better in every respect. In the two years it took Chevrolet to get the Camaro designed and into showrooms, auto journalists had a field day guessing what the Camaro would look like and how it would be built. Some predictions were reasonably accurate, some were miles off the mark.

The writers guessed wrong about the Camaro's basic construction. Nearly all assumed Chevrolet would give the Camaro a fully unitized (no frame) body. It made sense. The Mustang and its Falcon parent were both unitized. So was the Chevy II, which everyone assumed the Camaro would be based on.

But Chevrolet engineers weren't satisfied with the ride qualities of their Chevy II. Since the Chevy II was to be all-new for 1968, Chevrolet decided to design the 1967 Camaro first, then let the 1968 Chevy II share some Camaro components, not vice versa. This is an important distinction, because it means the 1967 Camaro was designed from scratch. It is true that some compromises were made knowing the Chevy II would later dip into the Camaro parts bin. Still, it was a lot less restrictive than having to design the Camaro around an existing chassis.

The chassis for the 1967 Camaro was semiunitized. It had a subframe in front but none in the rear. This wasn't unique (Mercedes had done the same), but it was different for a Camaro-class vehicle. By using this chassis design, Chevrolet managed to get the best of two worlds. The front subframe permitted strategically located rubber bushings to isolate front chassis components from the body in a way that gave Camaros, right from the start, the ride quality of much larger cars. With unitized rear construction, Camaros would still be produced and priced competitively. Unit construction is also more space-efficient, which maximizes trunk and rear seating space, both already in short supply in the stub-tailed Camaro design.

The name Camaro, by the way, was chosen by Chevrolet General Manager Elliott (Pete) Estes. Estes, who'd assumed the general manager's job at Chevrolet in July 1965, didn't care for the Panther name previously associated with Chevrolet's F-car program, and substituted Camaro at the last minute. He just liked the sound of it better.

Estes did take some journalistic heat for the selection. Chevrolet public relations said Camaro meant "comrade" or "pal" in French, but others found Spanish

This was the disappearing headlight trick, 1967 Camaro Rally Sport style. The grille styling of the Rally Sport versions of the first Camaros was indeed beautiful, but few people who viewed this famous Chevrolet photo took their eyes off the beautiful magician long enough to notice that the Camaro she leaned on was missing its hood script and turn-signal lamp. Chevrolet photo.

Ford's Mustang beat the Camaro into the marketplace by two and a half years, so when the Camaro was finally ready, Chevrolet pulled out all the stops for its introduction. Included in the promotional pizzazz were a full scale cutaway car complete with an exposed drivetrain, a simultaneous introduction of a women's clothing line called the Camaro Collection, and even a Camaro road race game for those Camaro buyers of the future. Chevrolet photos.

meanings ranging from "shrimp" to "loose bowels." That all died down, of course, and the Camaro name has stood the test of time beautifully.

Neither the Camaro, nor the way Chevrolet introduced it, could have disappointed many. For months before its release, Chevrolet advertising let word of the Camaro's coming-out reach the public. When it arrived on September 21, 1966, a half-hour movie, *The Camaro,* detailing the car's development and features, was shown in theaters and on TV. There was a Camaro stage revue called *Off Broadway* put on by four road companies around the country, and even a new line of women's clothing, the Camaro Collection, appeared in 400 shops nationwide.

Most important was the car, and the 1967 Camaro was an instant hit. It came in two body styles: a two-door coupe and a two-door convertible. The Camaro's coupe roofline was more fluid than the Mustang's coupe, which was one reason

This was the base Camaro for 1967, "base" meaning that it had neither Super Sport, Rally Sport or Z-28 equipment. Features to note in the front are the exposed headlights, grille-mounted turn signals and central grille emblem. The rear displayed a plain fuel cap and standard taillight assemblies with bright bezels and inboard-mounted backup lights. Chevrolet photos.

Chevrolet didn't find it necessary to offer a full fastback style to counter the Mustang's.

Within three months of introduction, six different engine displacements could be ordered. The base six-cylinder had 230 cubic inches and 140 horsepower. An optional six had 250-cubic-inch displacement, and 155 horsepower.

The range of V-8 power was delightful. The base V-8 (the Camaro was priced as a base six-cylinder coupe or convertible, or base V-8 coupe or convertible) had 327 cubic inches and 210 horsepower. An optional 327 had 275 horsepower. Also available was a 295-horsepower, 350-cubic-inch engine, a displacement that did not appear in any other Chevrolet product in 1967. The "big-block" made it into Camaros shortly after introduction in the form of the 396-cubic-inch, 325-horsepower motor, followed by a 375-horsepower variant of the same displacement. Last was the Z-28 package which included, among other things, a special 302-cubic-inch V-8 rated at 290 horsepower. Actually, the Z-28 made more like 375 horses in showroom trim. Set up for Trans-Am racing—which was what the Z-28 was intended for—the little 302 was good for an ear-splitting 450 horsepower.

Typical of the times, but not of ponycars, the standard Camaro transmission

This was the 1967 Camaro with both Super Sport and Rally Sport equipment. When these two options were combined, the SS emblems prevailed. The RS package included the special grille with electrically operated headlight covers (later years were vacuum), front turn signals mounted below the bumper, black inner bezels for the taillights and backup lights under the rear bumper. The car shown was an SS350, but if it had been an SS396, the grille and fuel-cap SS emblems would have had no numerical designation, and the rear body panel would have been painted dull black (except for black-exterior cars). Chevrolet photos.

The Custom Interior for 1967 featured a fancy seat pattern complete with contrasting color bands, and an inner door panel with molded-in arm-rest, recessed pocket for the door handle and carpeted bottom. Author photos.

1967 Camaro

BASE ENGINE (SIX CYLINDER)

Type: . . . . Chevrolet ohv inline 6
Bore x stroke, inches: 3.875x3.25
Displacement, inches: 230
Compression ratio: 8.5:1
Horsepower: . . . . 140 @ 4400 rpm
Torque: . . . . 220 @ 1600 rpm
Distributor: . . . . Single point breaker
Other engines offered: . . The optional six-cylinder engine was 250-cid with 155-hp. The base V-8 was 327-cid with 210-hp. Additional V-8 engines of 302-cid, 327-cid, 350-cid, and 396-cid were available with power ratings from 275-hp to 375-hp.

CHASSIS AND DRIVETRAIN

Clutch: . . . . Single dry-plate

Transmission: . . . Three-speed manual standard. Four-speed manual, two-speed automatic and three-speed automatic optional.
Front suspension: . . Coil springs, tube-type shock absorbers
Rear suspension: . . Leaf springs, tube-type shock absorbers
Axle ratio: . . . . 3.08:1 (other ratios available)
Frame: . . . . Box section front subframe, unibody rear

GENERAL

Wheelbase, inches: 108.0
Height, inches: 51.0
Width, inches: 72.5
Length, inches: 184.6
Brakes, standard: . . . . Drum
Wheels: . . . . Steel
Body material: . . . . Steel
Tire size, base: 7.35-14
Fuel capacity, gallons: 18.0

used a column-mounted, three-speed manual stick. You could pay extra for a floor shifter, or buy the between-the-seats console (RPO D55), which came with floor-mounted shifter. Or you could opt for the beefed-up three-speed manual (RPO M13), and you'd get a floor-mounted selector whether you wanted it or not.

There were wide-ratio (RPO M20) and close-ratio (RPO M21) four-speeds available. The optional automatic was the RPO M35 two-speed Powerglide, with the RPO M40 Turbo Hydramatic (Chevrolet spelled it Turbo Hydra-Matic in the early Camaro years) three-speed automatic available only with big-blocks. In 1967, just 1,453 Turbo Hydramatics were installed in Camaros.

The 1967 Camaro came with two interior trim levels: base and Custom. In a reversal of industry norm, both interiors included front bucket seats, but an *extra-cost* bench seat could be ordered with either, as could a fold-down rear seat.

Compared to the base interior, the Custom offered different seat patterns and inner door panels, molded trunk mat, glovebox light, deluxe steering wheel, underhood insulation and, on the coupes only, sail panel lamps and rear armrests with ashtrays.

A lesser Decor interior trim package could be ordered with either the base or Custom interior. It included bright metal pedal trim, bright windshield pillar moldings and bright roof rail moldings (the latter on coupes only).

Right from the start, Camaro offered its now famous and still confusing Super Sport (SS) and Rally Sport (RS) options. At first glance, the SS package looked like an engine deal, and the RS like extra trim. It wasn't that simple.

When introduced, the SS option was actually called SS350. It came only with the 350-cubic-inch engine, and that was the only way to order that engine. But it also included special hood ornaments, Bumble Bee paint stripe around the nose, nylon-cord red-stripe tires, six-inch wheels, SS fender emblems and SS350 emblems on the radiator grille and gas filler cap.

The RS option had a different grille (gorgeous) with electrically powered headlight covers, front parking lights located under the bumper, side paint stripes, front and rear wheelwell trim, roof drip gutter moldings (coupes), black inner taillight bezels, rear valance-mounted backup lights and RS emblems mounted on the radiator grille, fenders and gas filler cap.

Now the tricky part. For starters, the SS and RS could be ordered together. Where they overlapped (emblems, for instance) the SS items dominated. There was yet another exterior trim package, the Style Trim Group; this had side paint stripes, front and rear wheelwell trim and roof drip gutter moldings (coupes). But these things were already included in the RS package, so the Style Trim Group was an option only with the SS (provided it wasn't an RS, too) or with the base car.

There's more. Customers loved the SS Bumble Bee nose stripe, so it became a separate option in March 1967. In other words, a 1967 Camaro no longer needed to be an SS to get the stripe. And when the big-block engines came, it was mandatory to add the SS option. So there were SS350 and SS396 Camaros in 1967.

Another thing: You could get an upgraded steering wheel with either interior level, and a walnut-grain plastic rim was also optional.

The standard instrument setup had the speedometer in the left of two pods directly in front of the driver. In the right pod were fuel gauge and warning lights for the generator and coolant temperature. An optional gauge package (RPO U17) changed this considerably. The gauge option required the center console

Over the years, Camaros have been built in just two assembly plants, one in Norwood, Ohio, the other in Van Nuys, California. Interesting things to note in these Norwood factory photos are the cross-mounted muffler, single-leaf rear springs (criticized by magazine writers at the time) and front subframe with unitized rear construction. Chevrolet photos.

because the fuel, oil, temperature and battery gauges and clock were mounted in a cluster on the console. The right-side pod in front of the driver would then contain a 7000 rpm tachometer. The special instrumentation couldn't be ordered with six-cylinder engines, or with the stereo radio (which required an adapter that hung below the dash and wouldn't clear the console instruments).

The SS models and 1967 Camaros with 275-horsepower engines came with stiffer shocks and springs, but the same suspension could be ordered on any Camaro as option RPO F41. The F41 has been a familiar option through the Chevrolet line for years, and one that's always been money well spent. At $10.55 in the '67 Camaro, it was true again.

Nineteen sixty-seven Camaros came with manual steering as standard equipment, with power assist optional. The manual was slow with its 24:1 ratio, even

This was the base V-8 Camaro Sport Coupe for 1967. The flag emblems with 327 above them located on each front fender behind the wheelwells meant this Camaro had a 327-cubic-inch engine. The front antenna was standard equipment with all radios, but a rear mount could be specified for an extra $9.50. Whitewall tires were extra at $31.35 ($52 for nylon), and the RPO PO1 full wheelcovers cost another $21.10. Chevrolet photo.

The 1967 Camaro front and rear deck emblems stressed the Chevrolet origin, but in following years the emphasis reversed. Chevrolet photo.

No doubt about it, the Chevrolet lineup for 1967 was pretty impressive. This promotional photo shows the Corvair, Corvette, Chevy II, Chevelle, full-size Chevrolet and the new star of the show, the Camaro. The side pinstriping and rocker molding trim displayed on this prototype were not released for production. Chevrolet photo.

worse in the heavier convertibles or air-conditioned models at 28:1. Power steering dropped the ratio to 17.5:1. With both manual and power, RPO N44 (special fast steering) could drop the ratios further, to 18:1 and 15.6:1, respectively. Of all these, the faster power steering is probably the most desirable. But GM's power steering of that era emphasized low effort. It transmitted very little road feel back to the driver, something magazine test drivers complained about then, and something that still bothers me today. If you can put up with the extra effort, you might prefer the quick manual.

For stopping power, the standard drum brakes could be upgraded a couple of ways. The RPO J50 power brakes could be added. Metallic linings (RPO J65) could be specified for the drums. The RPO J52 included discs, but only in front. Finally, the rare RPO J56 option (just 205 sold) combined heavy-duty front discs with metallic linings for the rear drums.

Designers used the double-pod theme they knew was coming in the 1968 Corvette for their 1967 Camaro instrument panel. If equipped with the optional special instrumentation gauge package, a tachometer was placed in the right-side pod, which contained the fuel gauge in the standard arrangement. Since the special instrumentation included a secondary gauge cluster on the console, ordering the gauges meant ordering the optional console, too. An optional tape player for the radio mounted right under the ashtray and wouldn't clear the secondary gauge cluster, so these two options were incompatible. Author photos.

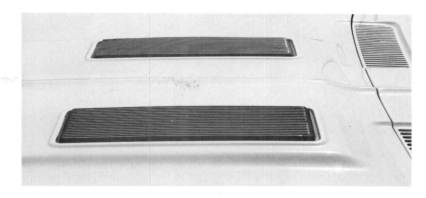

All 1967 Super Sport Camaros came with this special hood. The simulated "oil cooler" hood vents were not functional. Author photo.

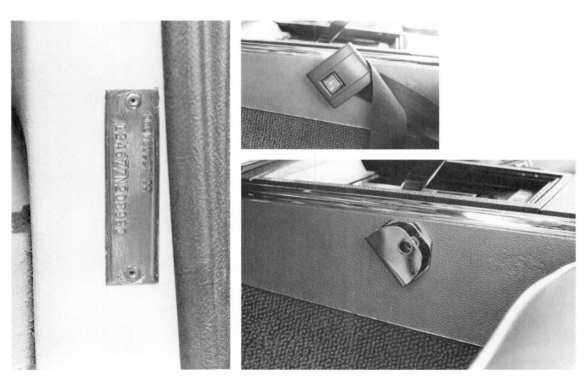

The 1967 Camaro's VIN (vehicle identification number) tag was riveted to the driver-side door post. This example, 124677N208960, translates to a V-8 convertible (12467), 1967 model (7), built at Norwood, Ohio (N). The six-digit number at the end increased by one for each car built. The console for the 1967 Camaro was unique to the year and had a handy little seatbelt-buckle storage receiver screwed into each side. Author photos.

Air conditioning has always been a Camaro option, but in 1967 less than thirteen percent had it. Only 2.2 percent had power windows. And cruise control made it into just 305 (0.1 percent) of the 220,906 1967 Camaros sold.

Let's take a hindsight look at how the 1967 Camaro compares to later years. It's the first Camaro, so that's important. Sometimes the first model of a series is plagued with ailments that make buying a later one more prudent. The Camaro first year wasn't perfect, but it has no stigma that should stop you from buying one. On the contrary, the first Camaros have outstanding durability and reliability records.

The only mechanical negatives you'll hear about the 1967 Camaros are their bottoming-out tendencies and rear wheel hop. The bottoming-out resulted from inadequate suspension travel and was improved in the 1968 model. It happened because the Camaro was originally designed with smaller wheels and tires, and more ground clearance. But these didn't give the designers the look they wanted, so bigger wheels and tires were substituted, and the car was lowered. Those two things conspired to eat up needed suspension travel. If you experience this problem today, all you need do is install adjustable air shocks that'll let you trim the car where you want it.

The rear wheel hop was caused, for the most part, by the combination of single-leaf rear springs and the near-vertical alignment of the rear shocks. The problem could occur on rough road surfaces when braking, but mostly it happened under hard, wheel-spinning acceleration. Chevrolet staggered the shocks in the 1968 model, and started using multi-leaf rear springs with the more potent engines. The 1967 Z-28 got a right-side radius rod to counter the wheel hop, but it was the only Z-28 to get that item factory-installed. Apparently, most or all SS350 and SS396 1967 Camaros also received the radius rod.

In anything close to normal driving, an owner of a 1967 Camaro won't experience wheel hop. But if it does present problems for your driving style, the later factory and across-the-counter improvements, including a traction bar, are bolt-on (except the staggered shocks) and can be retrofitted.

For a car designed over two decades ago, the 1967 Camaro is a surprisingly pleasant car to drive. It goes without saying that examples with potent engines will stand your hair on end, but even the more average ones are worthy of consideration as occasional or everyday transportation. Especially if you love attention.

In my opinion, today's new Camaro is the world's best enthusiast road car for the money. Even so, if you were to climb out of your brand-new Camaro into a 1967, the differences would not be drastic. You'd notice that the seats of the 1967 offer poor lateral support and no back rake adjustment. You'd like the feel behind the steering wheel, though the wheel's diameter would seem a little large at first. It would be apparent that the new Camaro had been given much more thought as to instrument and control locations, but you'd find the overall simplicity of the 1967 appealing.

Heating and defrosting systems have improved over the years, but the 1967's would present no problem whatever. In fact, they would work just as well as some of today's better-selling imports. The new Camaro's radio would sound better and the cabin would be quieter, but you'd love the responsiveness of the 1967 engine—any 1967 engine.

Vent windows disappeared from most GM cars in 1968, Camaros included. This makes the 1967 the only Camaro with vent windows. I wouldn't make a buy

Chevrolet offered four base-model Camaros in 1967: Sport Coupe with six-cylinder, Sport Coupe with V-8, convertible with six-cylinder and convertible with V-8. This car is a Sport Coupe with V-8. This was the most popular configuration, accounting for nearly 65 percent of 1967 production. Chevrolet photo.

or no-buy decision based on this alone, but given the choice, I'd sure prefer a car with them. They're great for arm-out-the-window driving.

If a 1967 is to be the Camaro you purchase, which models are the best investments? First, consider the obvious: Of the 220,906 Camaros sold in the 1967 model year, just 25,141 were convertibles. Considering Chevrolet didn't build any Camaro convertibles between 1970 and 1986, it makes sense that these are solid choices for appreciation. Those equipped wth lots of desirable options, big engines and nice trim are already expensive.

If you do decide on a convertible, be aware that just less than half had the optional power device to raise and lower the top. The power tops are worth more, but raising the manual top isn't all that difficult, and the simplicity of the manual system appeals to me, though I have heard that the hold-downs for the manual tops tend to break off.

The Z-28 came to life during the 1967 model run (December 1966). Only 602 were sold the first year, so this is an obvious big-money car. Good ones are already expensive, because it didn't take any genius to crystal-ball this one. The Z-28 will appeal to you most if you're a performance addict. It will continue to appreciate strongly because of its place in Camaro history, and because it's a terrific machine by any measure.

Of course, the Z-28 was built for performance, and a high percentage of the first year's production was sold to racers who didn't give a hoot about preserving the car or its original components. So, if you locate a pristine example, heaven knows how much it could someday be worth. I'd avoid a Z-28 that's been chopped up or seriously altered for racing, but cars with a documented racing history do have their market, too.

The Camaro was selected as the pace car for the Indianapolis 500 race in 1967. Chevrolet didn't make a few thousand replicas as is normal today, but it did

This was the base V-8 convertible for 1967. Oddly, Chevrolet elected to photograph this Camaro with standard blackwall tires and standard wheel discs, certainly not collector favorites today. At least it did have the Custom Interior. Of 220,906 Camaros made in 1967, 25,141 were convertibles, and just 5,285 were six-cylinder convertibles. Chevrolet photo.

1967 Camaro Colors/Options

Color Code	Body Color
AA	Tuxedo Black
CC	Ermine White
DD	Nantucket Blue
EE	Deepwater Blue
FF	Marina Blue
GG	Granada Gold
HH	Mountain Green
KK	Emerald Turquoise
LL	Tahoe Turquoise
MM	Royal Plum
NN	Madeira Maroon
RR	Bolero Red
SS	Sierra Fawn
TT	Capri Cream
YY	Butternut Yellow

INTERIOR COLORS: Black, Blue, Bright Blue, Gold, Parchment/Black, Red, Turquoise, Yellow

Order #	Item Description	Sticker $
12337	Base Camaro Sport Coupe, 6-cyl	2,466.00
12367	Base Camaro Convertible, 6-cyl	2,704.00
12437	Base Camaro Sport Coupe, V-8	2,572.00
12467	Base Camaro Convertible, V-8	2,809.00
AL4	Seat, Strato-Back Bench	26.35
AS1	Belts, Front Shoulder	23.20
AS2	Headrests, Strato-Ease	52.70
A01	Glass, Soft-Ray Tinted (all)	30.55
A02	Glass, Soft-Ray Tinted (windshield)	21.10
A31	Power Windows	100.10
A39	Belts, Custom Deluxe Front and Rear	6.35
A67	Seat, Folding Rear	31.60
A85	Belts, Custom Deluxe Front Shoulder	26.35
B37	Mats, Color-Keyed Floor	10.55
B93	Guards, Door Edge	3.20
C06	Power Convertible Top	52.70
C08	Roof Cover, Vinyl	73.75
C48	Heater and Defroster Deletion	−31.65
C50	Defroster, Rear Window	21.10
C60	Air Conditioning	356.00
D33	Mirror, Left Remote Control	9.50
D55	Console	47.40
D91	Band, Front End Accent	14.75
F41	Suspension, Special Purpose	10.55
G80	Axle, Positraction Rear	42.15
G94	Axle, Non-Standard Ratio (3.31:1)	2.15
G96	Axle, Non-Standard Ratio (3.55:1)	2.15
G97	Axle, Non-Standard Ratio (2.73:1)	2.15
H01	Axle, Non-Standard Ratio (3.07:1)	2.15
H05	Axle, Non-Standard Ratio (3.73:1)	2.15
J50	Power Brakes	42.15
J52	Brakes, Front Disc	79.00
J56	Brakes, Heavy-Duty Front Disc	105.35
J65	Brakes, Special Metallic Facing	36.90
K02	Fan, Temperature Controlled	15.80
K19	Air Injector Reactor (California)	44.75
K24	Ventilation, Closed Engine Positive	5.25
K30	Speed and Cruise Control	50.05

Order #	Item Description	Sticker $
K76	Generator, 61-Amp Delcotron	21.10
K79	Generator, 42-Amp Delcotron	10.55
L22	Engine, 155-hp, 250-cid 6-cyl	26.35
L30	Engine, 275-hp, 327-cid V-8	92.70
L35	Camaro Super Sport (w/325-hp)	263.30
L48	Camaro Super Sport (w/295-hp)	210.65
L78	Camaro Super Sport (w/375-hp)	500.30
M11	Shift Lever, Floor Mounted	10.55
M13	Transmission, Special 3-Speed	79.00
M20	Transmission, 4-Speed Wide Range	184.35
M21	Transmission, 4-Speed Close Ratio	184.35
M35	Transmission, Powerglide (w/6-cyl)	184.35
M35	Transmission, Powerglide (w/V-8)	194.35
M40	Transmission, Turbo Hydra-Matic	226.45
N10	Dual Exhaust System	21.10
N30	Steering Wheel, Deluxe	7.40
N33	Steering Wheel, Comfortilt	42.15
N34	Steering Wheel, Walnut-Grained	31.60
N40	Power Steering	84.30
N44	Steering, Quick Response	15.80
N61	Dual Exhaust System	21.10
N96	Wheel Covers, Mag-Style	73.75
PQ2	Tires, 7.35-14 Whitewall (nylon)	52.00
PW6	Tires, D70-14 Red Stripe	62.50
P01	Wheel Covers, Bright Metal	21.10
P02	Wheel Covers, Simulated Wire	73.75
P12	Wheels, Five 14''x6''	5.30
P58	Tires, 7.35-14 Whitewall	31.35
T60	Battery, Heavy-Duty	7.40
U03	Horn, Tri-Volume	13.70
U15	Speed Warning Indicator	10.55
U17	Instrumentation, Special	79.00
U25	Light, Luggage Compartment	2.65
U26	Light, Underhood	2.65
U27	Light, Glove Compartment	2.65
U28	Light, Ash Tray	2.65
U29	Lights, Courtesy	4.25
U35	Clock, Electric	15.80
U57	Stereo Tape System	128.50
U63	Radio, Pushbutton AM	57.40
U69	Radio, Pushbutton AM-FM	133.80
U73	Antenna, Rear Manual	9.50
U80	Speaker, Rear Seat	13.90
V01	Radiator, Heavy-Duty	10.55
V31	Guards, Front Bumper	12.65
V32	Guards, Rear Bumper	9.50
Z21	Style Trim Group	40.05
Z22	Rally Sport Package	105.35
Z23	Special Interior Group	10.55
Z28	Special Performance Package	358.10
Z28	Spec Perf Pkg (w/Exhaust Headers)	779.40
Z28	Spec Perf Pkg (w/Headers & Air Plenum)	858.40
Z87	Custom Interior	94.80

• Feature groups were available that combined appearance, lighting, and convenience items that are listed separately.
• Prices shown were introductory retail.

If you demand good old vent windows in your collectible Camaro, your model-year choices are limited to one. The 1967 was the only Camaro to have them. Author photo.

The Camaro was honored as the Indianapolis 500 Pace Car in 1967. But Chevrolet didn't build replicas for sale to the public in the same manner it often does today, and 1967 Camaro Pace Cars didn't appear in new-car ordering guides at Chevy dealerships. Chevrolet built four special Camaro Pace Cars for the actual race, but also built approximately 100 look-alikes for use by race officials and dignitaries. After the race, the replicas were sold to the public as used cars. Who knows, maybe Chevrolet built a few more on special order, though this officially didn't happen. All 1967 Pace Car replicas were white SS/RS convertibles with Bright Blue Custom Interiors. The real ones are collector prizes today. Author photo.

build about a hundred for use by race officials and dignitaries. After the race, Chevrolet sold them as used cars. They are, without question, very sought after now. These were 350- or 396-cubic-inch, SS-RS white convertibles with blue trim.

Beyond these obvious categories—convertibles, Z-28's and Pace Cars—you'll have to do some interpolation. Assuming the price you pay reflects condition, all high-performance Camaros of the first generation are sure to appreciate. This will continue, but we'll also see cars thought of as mundane creeping in. One reason ultra-high-performance cars of the sixties and early seventies have been so strong in the collector market is that Detroit didn't build anything even close in performance for several years. In time, Detroit rediscovered high performance. It's different now—computers, black boxes and all—so the simplicity and brute power of all musclecars will keep them valuable. But they might not continue to escalate in value as dramatically. Or at least the price gap between the powerhouses and the pussycats of the same model should tighten.

There were so many possible combinations of factory and dealer options and colors that it was statistically possible for every Camaro built in 1967 to be different in some slight way. They weren't all different, of course, but the point is that many beautiful automobiles, in option content and appearance, were built. It will be up to you to pick one that will out-pace the pack.

Personally, I never met a Rally Sport I didn't like . . . .

CHAPTER 2
1968 Camaro

SS350 ✪✪✪✪

SS396 ✪✪✪✪

Z-28 ✪✪✪✪✪

Add ✪ for Rally Sport

Add ✪ for convertible

1968 Model Production: 235,147

Camaros didn't *look* as if they'd changed much in 1968. The sheet metal did carry over almost intact, but there were differences between 1967 and 1968 Camaros; some minor, some not.

When you see a first-generation Camaro with vent windows, you know it's a 1967. When you see the same body style without them, it's a 1968. The 1969 is described in the following chapter, but I should say here that it had a lot of exterior sheet metal unique to it, and it looked quite different, even though many people think of 1967-69 Camaros as being the same. When the first Camaro came along, some criticized its soft, almost elegant design. To counter that, the 1969 got a more angular, muscular look, most evident in its squared-off wheelwells.

Beyond vent windows, there were other visual differences between the 1968 Camaro and its predecessor. Uncle Sam proclaimed side-marker lights mandatory for 1968 cars, so the Camaro got them. The grille of non-Rally Sport 1968 Camaros was restyled with a more pronounced center split. The 1968 Camaro taillights were housed in bezels that had a center divider the 1967's lacked. If it was a 1968 Rally Sport, all tail lamps within the bezels were red, the backup lights being mounted in the valance panel under the bumper. But if it wasn't a Rally Sport, the inboard lamps within the bezels were white and served the backup light function.

The major interior and exterior trim packages continued, but with a few modifications. Side pinstriping had been part of the Rally Sport in 1967, but had to be ordered separately in 1968. And the 1968 pinstriping followed the side character line instead of the fender peaks as before. The RS emblems were also restyled.

If you bought the SS350 in 1968, it came with the same hood as all 1967 Super Sports. But in 1968, the SS396 came with its own unique hood that featured two banks of nonfunctional intake ports, four per side. The rear taillight-surround panel of SS396 models was painted semi-gloss black in 1968, unless the car's exterior was black. In that case, the panel remained gloss-black like the rest of the body.

The wraparound Bumble Bee nose stripe continued as part of the SS packages and could be ordered separately, which was also true of 1967 models after March 1967. But two other nose treatments came along in 1968. One wrapped across the top of the nose, down the leading edge of the front fender to a point about

At first glance, the 1968 Camaro looked like the 1967, but look again. The non-Rally Sport grille was new, with a more pronounced taper off the center. The side vent windows were gone from the doors. And side-marker lamps, deemed necessary by Uncle Sam, appeared both front and rear. Chevrolet photo.

The clean look of the Rally Sport option remained for 1968, and 40,977 Rally Sport Camaros were sold that year. Engine displacements were indicated at the leading edge of the front fenders of all 1968 Camaros except for those with the base 230-cubic-inch, six-cylinder engine. Chevrolet photo.

four inches above the bumper, then horizontally back to almost the end of the door. The third nose treatment was multicolored and came as part of a Customized Camaro package offered during a sales promotion for part of the year. This required selecting one of four new exterior colors: Rallye Green, Brite Green, Corvette Bronze or LeMans Blue.

The engine lineup remained much the same as the year previous, but aluminum cylinder heads could be ordered with the RPO L78, 396-cubic-inch-displacement engine. The horsepower rating remained the same (375), though the RPO L89 aluminum head option included a different four-barrel carburetor. Just 272 Camaros received these special heads, which were also used sparingly on Corvettes, starting in 1967. These are rare and expensive today, but expansion of the aluminum did cause leakage problems. They're not the best for daily-use reliability.

An odd Camaro option available on 1968 (and 1969) models was called the Torque Drive transmission. This was a Powerglide that couldn't shift itself. The driver did the shifting manually, meaning he could start in first and shift to second, or just start in second if there wasn't any hurry. There was no clutch, the selectors were all column-mounted, and this option could be ordered only with the six-cylinder engines. A total of 3,099 of these manual-automatics, coded RPO M11, were fitted to 1968 Camaros.

Two interior grade levels continued to be offered: the standard no-cost and the extra-cost Custom. Both had newly styled door panels and seat upholstery designs. With the Custom, the color accents present in the 1967 model were no longer used. All the seat vinyls were "expanded" grade, meaning they were thicker and softer due to tiny air bubbles captured in the vinyl during manufacture. There was also a woven-cloth seat insert in a hound's-tooth black and white checked pattern.

The instrument panel was similar to the 1967's, but there were changes. First, the optional between-the-seats console was a completely new design, as were the optional instruments mounted on it. Where the 1967's optional instrument package was a straight-across cluster of three round faces (actually holding five instruments, including a clock), the 1968's was a sawtooth grouping of four rectangular instruments, two stacked above two more. The eliminated fifth dial was the clock, so designers ingeniously put one in the center of the tachometer in the right-side main dash pod, and created the Tick-Tock-Tach. That wasn't a name enthusiasts cooked up later; Chevrolet thought of it and used it, even in the 1968 owners manual.

In the 1967 Camaro, there were round air outlets at the corners of the dash in air-conditioned models. But in 1968 Camaros, the vent windows gone, there were round air-outlet ports in all dashes. The air-conditioned cars still used them, and non-air-conditioned models had them for the Astro Ventilation system. With the Astro system, outside air entered through the cowl and exited through exhaust holes in the door jambs. With this, GM reasoned, you didn't need to put the windows down, so you didn't need vent windows. Ha, ha!

It was in 1968 that Camaros first used five-leaf rear springs to replace the single-leaf springs born of the Chevy II. As mentioned, the single leaf was partly responsible for the wheel hop problem of the 1967 Camaro, but since this almost never happened except under hard acceleration, Chevrolet saw no reason to worry about Camaros unlikely to be driven hard. So the six, the 210-horsepower, 327-cubic-inch V-8 and the 275-horsepower, 327-cubic-inch V-8 with automatic

Here's a good comparison of the Rally Sport front versus the standard treatment. The Rally Sport had its hidden headlights and below-the-bumper turn signals as before. The RS center grille emblem was used only if it was a non-Super Sport. The standard front end shown is an SS350, but the center SS emblem didn't contain the 350 numbers as the 1967's did. The grille itself was new with a more pointed center. In production cars, the Bumble Bee stripe was interrupted for the displacement numbers. Chevrolet photos.

The rear of the 1968 Rally Sport Camaro was nearly identical to the 1967, but all 1968 Camaros had new taillight bezels with center dividers that effectively created a four-lamp look. Chevrolet photo.

1968 Camaro Colors/Options

Color Code	Body Color
AA	Tuxedo Black
CC	Ermine White
DD	Grotto Blue
EE	Fathom Blue
FF	Island Teal
GG	Ash Gold
HH	Grecian Gold
JJ	Rallye Green
KK	Tripoli Turquoise
LL	Teal Blue
NN	Cordovan Maroon
OO	Corvette Bronze
PP	Seafrost Green
RR	Matador Red
TT	Palomino Ivory
UU	Le Mans Blue
VV	Sequoia Green
YY	Butternut Yellow
ZZ	Brittish Green

INTERIOR COLORS: Black, Blue, Gold, Red, Turquoise, Parchment/Black, Black/White

Order #	Item Description	Sticker $
12337	Base Camaro Sport Coupe, 6-cyl	2,565.00
12367	Base Camaro Convertible, 6-cyl	2,802.00
12437	Base Camaro Sport Coupe, V-8	2,670.00
12467	Base Camaro Convertible, V-8	2,908.00
AK1	Belts, Custom Deluxe Seat and Shoulder	11.10
AL4	Seat, Strato-Back Bench	32.65
AS1	Belts, Front Shoulder	23.20
AS2	Headrests, Strato-Ease	52.70
AS4	Belts, Custom Deluxe Rear Shoulder	26.35
AS5	Belts, Standard Rear Shoulder	23.20
A01	Glass, Soft-Ray Tinted (all)	30.55
A02	Glass, Soft-Ray Tinted (windshield)	21.10
A31	Power Windows	100.10
A39	Belts, Custom Deluxe Front and Rear	7.90
A67	Seat, Folding Rear	42.15
A85	Belts, Custom Deluxe Front Shoulder	26.35
B37	Mats, Color-Keyed Floor	10.55
B93	Guards, Door Edge	4.25
C06	Power Convertible Top	52.70
C08	Roof Cover, Vinyl	73.75
C50	Defroster, Rear Window (w/Sp Cpe)	21.10
C50	Defroster, Rear Window (w/Conv)	31.60
C60	Air Conditioning	360.20
D33	Mirror, Left Remote Control	9.50
D55	Console	50.60
D80	Spoiler	32.65
D90	Striping, Sport	25.30
D91	Band, Front End Accent	14.75
D96	Striping, Accent	13.70
F41	Suspension, Special Purpose	10.55
G31	Springs, Special Rear	20.05
G80	Axle, Positraction Rear	42.15
—	Axle, Optional Ratios	2.15
J50	Power Brakes	42.15
J52	Brakes, Front Disc	100.10
KD5	Ventilation, Closed Engine Positive HD	6.35
K02	Fan, Temperature Controlled	15.80
K30	Speed and Cruise Control	52.70
K76	Generator, 61-Amp Delcotron	26.35

Order #	Item Description	Sticker $
K79	Generator, 42-Amp Delcotron	10.55
L30	Engine, 275-hp, 327-cid V-8	92.70
L34	Camaro Super Sport (w/350-hp)	368.65
L35	Camaro Super Sport (w/325-hp)	263.30
L48	Camaro Super Sport (w/295-hp)	210.65
L78	Camaro Super Sport (w/375-hp)	500.30
L89	Camaro Super Spt (w/375-hp & Alum Hds)	868.95
MB1	Transmission, Torque-Drive	68.65
M11	Shift Lever, Floor Mounted	10.55
M13	Transmission, Special 3-Speed	79.00
M20	Transmission, 4-Speed Wide Ratio	184.35
M21	Transmission, 4-Speed Close Ratio	184.35
M22	Transmission, 4-Speed Close Ratio HD	310.70
M35	Transmission, Powerglide (w/6-cyl)	184.35
M35	Transmission, Powerglide (w/V-8)	194.35
M40	Transmission, Turbo Hydra-Matic	237.00
NF2	Dual Exhaust System, Deep-Tone	27.40
N10	Dual Exhaust System	27.40
N30	Steering Wheel, Deluxe	4.25
N33	Steering Wheel, Comfortilt	42.15
N34	Steering Wheel, Walnut-Grained	31.60
N40	Power Steering	84.30
N44	Steering, Quick Response	15.80
N65	Tire, Space Saver Spare	19.35
N95	Wheel Covers, Simulated Wire	73.75
N96	Wheel Covers, Mag-Style	73.75
PA2	Wheel Covers, Mag-Spoke	73.75
PW7	Tires, F70-14 Whitewall	64.75
PW8	Tires, F70-14 Red Stripe	64.75
PY4	Tires, F70-14 White Stripe (Belted)	26.55
PY5	Tires, F70-14 Red Stripe (Belted)	26.55
P01	Wheel Covers, Bright Metal	21.10
P58	Tires, 7.35-14 Whitewall	31.35
T60	Battery, Heavy-Duty	7.40
U03	Horn, Tri-Volume	13.70
U15	Speed Warning Indicator	10.55
U17	Instrumentation, Special	94.80
U35	Clock, Electric	15.80
U46	Light Monitoring System	26.35
U57	Stereo Tape System	133.80
U63	Radio, Pushbutton AM	61.10
U69	Radio, Pushbutton AM-FM	133.80
U73	Antenna, Rear Manual	9.50
U79	Radio, Pushbutton AM-FM Stereo	239.15
U80	Speaker, Rear Seat	13.20
V01	Radiator, Heavy-Duty	13.70
V31	Guard, Front Bumper	12.65
V32	Guard, Rear Bumper	12.65
ZJ7	Wheels, Rally	31.60
ZJ9	Lighting, Auxiliary (Sp Cpe w/Z87)	11.10
ZJ9	Lighting, Auxiliary (Sp Cpe w/o Z87)	13.70
ZJ9	Lighting, Auxiliary (Conv w/Z87)	6.85
ZJ9	Lighting, Auxiliary (Conv w/o Z87)	9.50
Z21	Style Trim Group	42.15
Z22	Rally Sport Package	105.35
Z23	Special Interior	17.95
Z28	Special Performance Package	400.25
Z87	Custom Interior	110.60

• Appearance and convenience groups were available that combined items listed separately above.
• Prices shown were introductory retail.

Hey, what better way to tell folks about the 1968 Camaro's new hound's-tooth-check seat upholstery than to photograph it in the company of this lovable fellow? Chevrolet photo.

1968 Camaro

BASE ENGINE (SIX CYLINDER)
Type: . . . . Chevrolet ohv inline 6
Bore x stroke, inches: 3.875x3.25
Displacement, inches: 230
Compression ratio: 8.5:1
Horsepower: . . . . 140 @ 4400 rpm
Torque: . . . . 220 @ 1600 rpm
Distributor: . . . . Single point breaker
Other engines offered: . . The optional six-cylinder engine was 250-cid with 155-hp. The base V-8 was 327-cid with 210-hp. Additional V-8 engines of 302-cid, 327-cid, 350-cid, and 396-cid were available with power ratings from 275-hp to 375-hp.

CHASSIS AND DRIVETRAIN
Clutch: . . . . Single dry-plate

Transmission: . . . Three speed manual standard. Four-speed manual, two-speed automatic and three-speed automatic optional.
Front suspension: . . Coil springs, tube-type shock absorbers
Rear suspension: . . Leaf springs, tube-type shock absorbers
Axle ratio: 3.08:1
Frame: . . . . Box section front subframe, unibody rear

GENERAL
Wheelbase, inches: 108.0
Height, inches: 51.5
Width, inches: 72.6
Length, inches: 184.7
Brakes, standard: . . . . Drum
Wheels: . . . . Steel
Body material: . . . . Steel
Tire size, base: 7.35-14
Fuel capacity, gallons: 18.5

transmission had to get along with the single-leaf springs. But in the effort to make the Camaro all things to all people, RPO C31 would get you the multi-leaf springs for $20.05 on any 1968 Camaro.

A big suspension improvement all 1968 Camaros *did* receive was staggered rear shocks. Angling the shocks so the passenger-side one passed behind the axle, and the driver-side one ahead of it, did wonders for the wheel hop blues. And all 1968 Camaros got additional suspension travel to help the bottoming-out problems of 1967.

No 1968 Camaro left the factory with four-wheel disc brakes. Intended for the Z-28 models, they were sold across the counter.

Nineteen sixty-eight could be called the year of the Z-28, because it really came into its own that year. The Z-28 came along as a delayed option package for the 1967 model. Individuals did buy it for the street, but Chevrolet had designed the Z-28 as a racer and wasn't even sure it wanted to sell it to the public. In 1967, Chevrolet didn't advertise the Z-28 for public consumption, but the car got plenty of advertising on its own with surprisingly strong showings in the Trans-Am racing series (surprising considering it was the Camaro's first year).

Though similar in layout, the 1968 interior did differ from that of 1967. The optional console was brand-new. This photo shows a Custom Interior, and for 1968 that meant new seat and door panel designs, woodgraining on the dash and a passenger grab bar over the glovebox door. The car shown also had the Tick-Tock-Tach, a combination clock and tachometer solution to a not-enough-holes-in-the-dash dilemma created by the 1968 Camaro's new secondary instrument cluster design. Also, 1968 was the year of Astro Ventilation, and the round air entry ports can be seen at each end of the dash. Chevrolet photo.

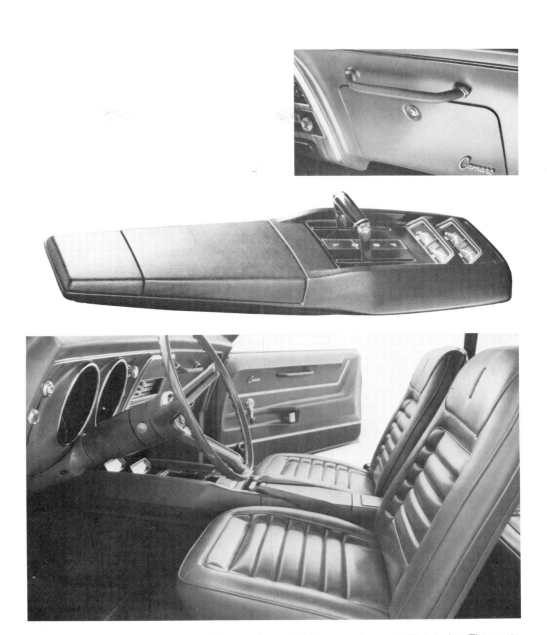

Here are different views of things new to the 1968 interior. The seats were the Custom Interior variety and they didn't have contrasting color bands as 1967's did. The console was all-new, as was the staggered "sawtooth" secondary instrument cluster mounted on it. If you ordered Special Instrumentation in 1968, you got the four instruments mounted on the console (console purchase required, obviously) plus the tachometer/clock combination in the right-side dash pod in front of the driver. If you skipped the instrumentation but still wanted a clock, it was mounted by itself on the console. The passenger grab handle came with the Custom Interior or Special Interior groups. Chevrolet photos.

This was the Z-28 for 1968. Its muscle was in its motor and chassis, including such standard items as the special 302-cubic-inch engine, dual low-restriction mufflers, special suspension front and rear, heavy-duty radiator with temperature-controlled fan, and six-inch wheels with fifteen-inch nylon tires. There were more exterior clues to this car's intent, the most prominent being bold hood and rear deck stripes. The rear spoiler was a common sight on Z-28 Camaros, but was a separate option available on any model (15,520 spoilers were sold in 1968). The car shown had Z-28 identification on its front fenders, but some 1968 Z-28 models had just the 302 numerals instead. Remember that initially the Z-28 was nothing more than an order code. But the Z-28 name had a special ring to it, magazines and customers started using it, so Chevrolet went with it. Chevrolet photo.

Another factor in the Z-28 self-advertising was the response of auto journalists who were ecstatic over it.

In 1968, Chevrolet decided to roll with the flow and start promoting the Z-28 for street use. Mark Donohue, driving for Roger Penske and with considerable covert factory assistance, walked away with the Trans-Am series, winning ten of thirteen races. The Z-28 was on the map!

Nineteen sixty-seven Z-28 production was 602, with a good percentage going right to the racetrack. In 1968, production leaped to 7,199, so many more went into the hands of nonracers. There are street-driven Z-28 Camaros of the 1968 vintage to be had. Considering the historical impact of Donohue's Trans-Am domination, beautiful styling and the inherent value of these machines, they are tremendous investments.

If comparing 1967 and 1968 models for desirability now, they rate a tossup. The 1967 has the advantage of being the first Camaro, which is always important in any successful series of cars. Very few unmolested Z-28's remain, but those that do are very valuable. Again, the Z-28's were the first of a model designation still held in high esteem today. Nineteen sixty-seven models did have a few teething problems, mainly in the rear suspension. But these are not normally noticed in everyday driving, and can be corrected with the addition of later components if the owner so chooses.

On the 1968 side of the equation, suspension improvements were designed in. The interior materials are a little nicer and more livable. Assembly of any car gets better the second year of a similar design, as rattles get taken care of and engineers generally get down to the fine-tuning details. The overall numbers sold were similar—220,906 1967 models compared to 235,147 in 1968—so that's not a factor.

If you're leaning toward a first-generation (1967-69) Camaro, first look carefully at a 1967-68, then at a 1969. The 1969 is quite different and many Camaro enthusiasts fall into its camp, or that of the earlier two years, but not both. If your preference is the cleaner styling of the 1967-68 models, selection of a 1968 means you value its slightly better construction and engineering more highly than the 1967's vent windows or historical "first Camaro" status.

CHAPTER 3
1969 Camaro

1969 Model Production: 243,085

★★★

★★★(SS350

★★★★ SS396

★★★★(Pace Car

★★★★★ Z-28, COPO 427

Add (for convertible

We won't get all Camaro enthusiasts to agree which Camaro year was the all-around best. But if it was put to a vote, the 1969 would be a contender. Let's see if we can determine why.

For starters, the 1969 stands out as the most nearly unique single Camaro model year. It was part of the first generation (1967-69) and shared the same chassis. But in the sixties, U.S. cars seldom went more than two years without a major facelift. Even though the 1970 Camaro was going to be all-new, Chevrolet felt compelled to change the 1969 substantially.

This model set a Camaro sales record, 243,085, that stood until 1978. But it was a longer-than-usual model year, extending from a normal introduction date of September 26, 1968, to February 26, 1970. This was because the 1970 models were late.

Because Chevrolet called its 1970 model a 1970½, some people assume that late 1969's are actually 1970 Camaros. Some dealers did title them that way (and some got sued for doing it), but a 1969 is a 1969, and a 1970 is a 1970, and that's all there is to it. Even the Chevrolet dealer price guides called the 1969 body style a 1969 right up until the new body style was announced.

Back to uniqueness: To counter criticism that the first Camaro didn't look aggressive enough, the 1969 got considerable new sheet metal, including header, valance, fenders, doors, rear quarters and rear end panel. The Camaro identity was still there, but it surely looked different. The wheelwells were flattened out at the tops, and lips formed and flowed off each wheelwell, a theme said to have been borrowed from the Mercedes-Benz 300-SL. Rear panels were new to accept wider taillight bezels, each with a triple-lens look to replace the earlier double treatment. The standard grille was redesigned with sharper angles, and the headlights interrupted the grille in a way that made the lights more pronounced. In the Rally Sport, the headlights were still hidden, but this time the covering doors each had three peephole slits, so the lights would shine through if the doors didn't open. (You couldn't see beans if this happened, but at least other cars could see you.) The peephole doors and grille design didn't harmonize as previous Rally Sport grilles did.

The net result of reworking the exterior of the 1969 was a much meaner, more aggressive look. The designers sought to make the Camaro look as if it meant business just standing still.

The interior took on a new appearance as well. The entire instrument panel was new, but the Camaro's basic theme of two big pods in front of the driver re-

Many Camaros excite enthusiasts, but the 1969 has been the hottest in the collector marketplace in recent memory. And no wonder. It was the last of the first generation. The option list was the longest of any Camaro before or since. The model shown is a Rally Sport convertible. The thin fender striping was part of the Rally Sport deal in 1969, unless sport striping or the Z-28 was ordered with it. Chevrolet photos.

mained intact. In 1969, these big pods became almost square, in contrast to the previous round dials. In the standard arrangement, the speedometer remained in the left pod, the fuel gauge in the right. With the optional instruments, the stacked cluster for fuel, oil pressure, water temperature and ammeter stayed on the optional console, which itself remained essentially unchanged from 1968. The tach went into the big pod to the right, in front of the driver as before, but the clock went to a new position between the big pods. The new arrangement permitted the clock to become a separate option, available in any Camaro. However, if the tachometer was ordered without the optional cluster stack, the fuel gauge occupied the center pod, not allowing the clock to be placed there.

The air outlets for Astro Ventilation became rectangular for 1969; one was located at each end of the dash. Air-conditioned cars also used these vents, along with a double vent in the center of the dash.

Two levels of interiors continued, with changes for the sake of change in embossing patterns, trim and color availability. As in 1968, the base interior was

Enthusiasts and collectors agree that the 1969 instrument panel, which was new in 1969 and exclusive to that year, has stood the test of time well. The twin-pod theme continued, but with a stronger, more aggressive tone much in keeping with the overall redesign of the 1969. Chevrolet photo.

Here's the standard (non-Rally Sport) front and rear treatment for 1969. Single headlights boldly interrupted a coarse grille mesh in front. At the rear, new taillights took on a triple-segmented look. The backup lights were incorporated into the center taillight section, except for Rally Sports which had the backup lights mounted under the bumper. Chevrolet photos.

The headlights in Rally Sports again hid behind doors when not in use, but in 1969 the doors had peephole slits in them. The center grille section was a subdued black plastic. The RS grille emblem was new for 1969, but when combined with the Super Sport, the SS emblems were used instead. Chevrolet photo.

This breakaway display nicely showed the first-generation Camaro's front subframe. The display signs included phrases like, "Who needs to say 'sportier?' Who could? Just decide on the Camaro that fits your budget and sportsided imagination," "To come this close to a Corvette, we picked the best sports car brains around. Our own," and "This is the spirited way to challenge a road and not your wallet." Chevrolet photo.

vinyl only, the Custom either vinyl or hound's-tooth-check cloth. More hound's-tooth-check cloth colors were added.

The real news was engine availability. Not all were on the option sheets simultaneously, but before the year was finished no fewer than fourteen different engines were factory installed. That's another Camaro record!

First the easy part: The 140- and 155-horsepower six-cylinder engines remained in the lineup as before. Now to the V-8's: At the start of production, the base V-8 was the 210-horsepower, 327-cubic-inch engine, the same as in 1967 and 1968. But this was dropped, and a new 307-cubic-inch engine of 200 horsepower replaced it. There were 250- and 300-horsepower versions of the 350-incher, and four different 396 possibilities, if you counted the RPO L89 aluminum cylinder head option as a separate motor, which it was.

There was another engine that made it into 1969 Camaros—the ZL-1. If ever a killer Camaro existed, this was it. The ZL-1 option was no less than a full-race, aluminum-block, 427-cubic-inch drag racer. At an additional $4,160, this option came to more than the Camaro's base price. Just sixty-nine of these fire-breathers

Chevrolet sold 20,302 Z-28 Camaros in 1969 and here's the big reason why. Actually, the small reason why. Out of just 302 cubic inches, Chevy engineers pulled a thundering 290 horsepower, conservatively rated at that. Of course, the Z-28 offered much more, including dual exhausts, bumper guards, heavy-duty radiator and temperature-controlled fan, quick-ratio steering, 15x7-inch wheels with E70x15 special white-letter tires and special paint stripes. Not bad for $458.15, or $473.95, or $522.40, depending on when during the long 1969 Camaro model year you placed your order. Author photo.

were built. Many people think this was the fastest American production car of all time. The ZL-1 Camaros may also be the most valuable Camaros in existence. How did they come to be? Chevrolet bends over backward to please its dealers and customers, and in 1969 it was also keeping its eyes open for anything that enhanced the Camaro's performance image. So when Illinois Chevrolet dealer Fred Gibb asked Chevrolet to build him fifty ZL-1 Camaros (fifty to qualify it for NHRA drag racing), Chevrolet obliged. Some other dealers heard about this special run and put their own orders in, so the total was sixty-nine ZL-1 Camaros built. They came down the regular Camaro production line, but were pulled off to the side for their special engine installations.

An RPO number was never assigned to the ZL-1 option. RPO means Regular Production Option, and there wasn't anything "regular" about these beasts. No, these went under the heading of COPO (Central Office Production Order) 9560.

Along the same line as the ZL-1 Camaros were the iron-block L-72 Camaros. Just as Fred Gibb had done, dealer-racer Don Yenko asked Chevrolet to factory-assemble 427-cubic-inch-displacement Camaros for his Yenko super-car dealership. These were built under COPO 9561. There were 201 Yenko Camaros built by Chevrolet in 1969 but, just as with ZL-1 Camaros, other dealers got wind of the Yenkos and additional iron-block 427 Camaros were built under COPO 9561. The exact number isn't known.

These COPO Camaros are valuable collector items today, but if you're in the market for one, make sure it's backed up with documentation since many dealer and amateur 427-engine installations have been done over the years.

Not too many people knew about COPO 9560 and 9561, but they sure knew about the Z-28 by 1969. The Donohue-Penske Camaro effort again captured the Trans-Am series title, and the Z simply became a premier performance car in an era filled with them. Chevrolet wisely didn't tamper excessively with its production Z-28 for 1969, but there were improvements, including four-bolt main bearings, which the 1969 350-cubic-inchers also received.

Famed Corvette designer Larry Shinoda came up with a neat new hood for high-performance 1969 Camaros. It featured a rear-facing, cold-air inlet similar to the 1967 Sting Rays with 427-cubic-inch engines. This cowl induction hood was included on all 427-engine Camaros in 1969, and was available as a regular production option for Z-28's and Super Sports. This hood was also made available over-the-counter by Chevrolet (in fiberglass) to fit the crossram carburetor setup, and also to fit the single four-barrel carburetor when a special adaptor piece was fitted.

One of the last Camaro complaints the magazine people had was taken away in 1969, when the Muncie four-speed shift linkage was replaced by one made by and prominently identified as Hurst.

The Camaro got the nod again in 1969 to pace the Indy 500 race. The car was a 375-horsepower, SS396 convertible with "hugger" orange racing stripes, rear spoiler and black-orange hound's-tooth-check cloth upholstery. This time Chevrolet made replicas available in quantity for sale to the public (RPO Z11), and 3,674 were sold.

The option sheet for the 1969 Camaro was very long. It's hard to imagine Chevrolet actually offered some of the things it did. The most nutball of all (and it wasn't unique to Camaros) was the so-called Traction Compound Dispenser. This was a remote-controlled can that squirted deicer on the rear tires so that nicely-dressed ladies wouldn't have to push their Camaros out of snowdrifts. I've

The Cobras of the Camaro world are the COPO cars. These Camaros never appeared on dealer order sheets, but were bonafide factory-built vehicles. The most awesome was the ZL-1, an aluminum-block, 427-cubic-inch street rocket with incredible power. Chevrolet thought about offering it as a regular production option complete with sinister graphics to match its mission, but decided against it. Chevrolet dealer Fred Gibb knew of the plans and asked Chevrolet to build him 50 ZL-1 Camaros to sell as drag racers. Chevrolet obliged (the number grew to 69 as other dealers jumped in), but the exterior graphics never made it. COPO 9560 ZL-1 Camaros looked like any other plain-Jane Camaro . . . until you lifted the hood. Another category of COPO Camaro was the Yenko. This was almost a repeat of the Gibb story, except this time the Chevy dealer was Don Yenko: The Camaros were iron-block L-72 427-cubic-inchers; 201 were built; and Yenko added his own exterior graphics to set these COPO 9561 Camaros apart. There were additional Camaros built under COPO 9561 for other dealers, but the quantity isn't known. If a COPO Camaro interests you (these are expensive!), be sure it's documented because amateur big-block installations were common. The car shown above is a genuine Yenko. Its graphics have been faithfully duplicated, but individual cars varied. This one had a tach, but no console, so the fuel gauge went into the center dash pod. Also, Yenko used 140-mph speedometers, factory installed, but usually destined for police cars. Author photos.

never seen one of these deicers in the flesh (not that I've been looking), so I can't tell you if they work or not. Since a total of only 188 people sprang for this out of nearly a quarter-million 1969 Camaros sold, it isn't too likely you'll see one, either.

The Rally Sport option continued, with detail differences. One meriting mention was the headlight-washing system. It came with the RS package, but could be ordered separately as RPO CE1 for $15.80. As with previous years, Rally Sports had different tail lamps with backup lamps below the bumper.

In the Super Sport department, the 396-engine models continued to include the dull-black rear end panel (again, not dull with black cars) and the special hood with eight horizontal, simulated intakes remained standard on all Super Sports.

Nineteen sixty-nine Camaros could be striped four different ways. The Z-28's (and Pace Car replicas) came with wide racing stripes on the hood and rear deck. Included with the Rally Sport were highlight stripes on the wheelwell brows. Standard with the Super Sport was a stripe that started with a vertical slash at the leading edge of the front fender, then trailed horizontally back into the door,

Here's the famous and oh-so-popular liquid tire chain option for 1969 Camaros. Chevrolet sold 243,085 Camaros in 1969, and a mere 188 had this ultra-rare RPO V75 option. Needless to say, it disappeared from the order forms the following year. Not that the concept, a dash-controlled aerosol can of ice-melter, was all that bad. Chevrolet photos.

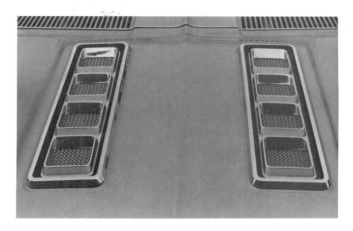

The quad-port, heavy-mesh hood trim came only with the SS396 in 1968, but was standard with all SS models in 1969. The design was created by Corvette stylist Larry Shinoda. Author photo.

A first-generation Camaro didn't seem like a Camaro without stripes of some kind, and in 1969 there were four varieties. This was the standard striping with SS models, but it could be ordered (RPO D90) with any Camaro except the Z-28 and Pace Car replica. Chevrolet photo.

stopping just above the door handle. The fourth possibility was a variant of the Bumble Bee, this one crossing the nose and sweeping back up the hood.

Power steering was optional, as usual, but in 1969 it was a new variable-ratio unit. This meant that as the wheels were turned from center, they turned progressively more as the steering wheel approached lock. The idea was to reduce the number of turns lock-to-lock without making steering too twitchy on the highway.

Four-wheel disc brakes (power) became a bona fide 1969 Camaro factory option. These brakes were adapted from the Corvette, and used the same four-pistons-per-wheel, fixed-caliper design. But the discs for the disc-drum Camaro brakes used a new single-piston, floating-caliper design. The four-wheel discs were only available with the Z-28 or Super Sport options. Chevrolet sales records show 206 sets were factory-installed in 1969 Camaros; more have been owner-installed. The Super Sport option was priced to include disc brakes up front. The Z-28 didn't include the brakes in its price, but either front discs or four-wheel discs were mandatory.

The Turbo Hydramatic three-speed automatic transmission was optional on some 1967 and 1968 Camaros, but on all in 1969 (except the Z-28 models, which were all four-speed manuals).

By now it should be evident why 1969 Camaros are viewed so positively today. This year simply had it all. The choice of engines, other options and colors (see charts) was magnificent. It was the last year until 1987 for Camaro convertibles, there was a Pace Car replica, those wonderful Z-28's, Super Sport and Rally Sport packages, the rare ZL-1 and L-72 central office jobs . . . if Chevrolet couldn't build the Camaro of your dreams in 1969, it never could. Unless, of course, you didn't like the looks of the 1969.

Styling is one of those subjective things very difficult to write about. In terms of pure styling elegance, my pick of the first generation would be a 1967-68 Rally Sport. Designers gewgawed the 1969 a little because they decided—or were told

---

1969 Camaro

BASE ENGINE (SIX CYLINDER)

Type: .Chevrolet ohv inline 6
Bore x stroke, inches: 3.85x3.25
Displacement, inches: 230
Compression ratio: 8.5:1
Horsepower: .140 @ 4400 rpm
Torque: .220 @ 1600 rpm
Distributor: . . . . .Single point breaker
Other engines offered: . .The optional six-cylinder engine was 250-cid with 155-hp. The base V-8 initially was the 327-cid with 210-hp as before, then changed to 307-cid with 200-hp. Additional V-8 engines of 302-cid 327-cid, 350-cid, and 396-cid were available with power ratings from 250-hp to 375-hp. Also, 427-cid V-8 engines were available as COPO (Central Office Production Order) options in both cast iron and aluminum blocks.

CHASSIS AND DRIVETRAIN

Clutch: . . . . .Single dry-plate
Transmission: . . .Three speed manual standard. Four-speed manual, two-speed automatic and three-speed automatic optional.
Front suspension: . .Coil springs, tube-type shock absorbers
Rear suspension: . .Leaf springs, tube-type shock absorbers
Axle ratio: 2.73:1
Frame: . . . . .Box section front subframe, unibody rear

GENERAL

Wheelbase, inches: 108.0
Height, inches: . . . . .51.1 (coupe,) 50.9 (conv)
Width, inches: 74.0
Length, inches: 186.0
Brakes, standard: . . . . .Drum
Wheels: . . . . .Steel
Body material: . . . . .Steel
Tire size, base: E78-14
Fuel capacity, gallons: 18.5

Code	Body Color	Code	Body Color
10	Tuxedo Black	61	Burnished Brown
40	Butternut Yellow	63	Champagne
50	Dover White	65	Olympic Gold
51	Dusk Blue	67	Burgundy
52	Garnet Red	69	Cortez Silver
53	Glacier Blue	71	Le Mans Blue
55	Azure Turquoise	72	Hugger Orange
57	Fathom Green	76	Daytona Yellow
59	Frost Green	79	Rallye Green
53/50	Glacier Blue/Dover White Two-Tone		
55/50	Azure Turquoise/Dover White Two-Tone		
53/51	Glacier Blue/Dusk Blue Two-Tone		
51/53	Dusk Blue/Glacier Blue Two-Tone		
65/50	Olympic Gold/Dover White Two-Tone		
61/63	Burnished Brown/Champagne Two-Tone		

INTERIOR COLORS: Black, Blue, Medium Green, Ivory/Black, Red, Midnight Green, Black Houndstooth, Ivory Houndstooth, Yellow Houndstooth, Orange Houndstooth

Order #	Item Description	Sticker $
12337	Base Camaro Sport Coupe, 6-cyl	2,621.00
12367	Base Camaro Convertible, 6-cyl	2,835.00
12437	Base Camaro Sport Coupe, V-8	2,727.00
12467	Base Camaro Convertible, V-8	2,940.00
AS1	Belts, Front Shoulder	23.20
AS4	Belts, Custom Deluxe Rear Shoulder	26.35
AS5	Belts, Standard Rear Shoulder	23.20
A01	Glass, Soft-Ray Tinted	32.65
A31	Power Windows	105.35
A39	Belts, Custom Deluxe Front and Rear	9.00
A67	Seat, Folding Rear	42.15
A85	Belts, Custom Deluxe Front Shoulder	26.35
B37	Mats, Color-Keyed Floor	11.60
B93	Guards, Door Edge	4.25
CE1	Headlight Washer	15.80
C06	Power Convertible Top	52.70
C08	Roof Cover, Vinyl	84.30
C50	Defroster, Rear Window (w/Sp Cpe)	22.15
C50	Defroster, Rear Window (w/Conv)	32.65
C60	Air Conditioning	376.00
DX1	Striping, Front Accent	25.30
D33	Mirror, Left Remote Control	10.55
D34	Mirror, Visor Vanity	3.20
D55	Console	53.75
D90	Striping, Sport	25.30
D96	Striping, Fender	15.80
F41	Suspension, Special Purpose	10.55
G31	Springs, Special Rear	20.05
G80	Axle, Positraction Rear	42.15
—	Axle, Optional Ratios	2.15
JL8	Brakes, Power 4-Wheel Disc	500.30
J52	Brakes, Power Front Disc	64.25
J50	Power Brakes	42.15
KD5	Ventilation, Closed Engine Positive HD	6.35
KO2	Fan, Temperature Controlled	15.80
KO5	Heater, Engine Block	10.55
K79	Generator, 42-Amp Delcotron	10.55
K85	Generator, 63-Amp Delcotron	26.35
LM1	Engine, 255-hp, 350-cid V-8	52.70
L22	Engine, 155-hp, 250-cid 6-cyl	26.35
L34	Engine, 350-hp, 396-cid V-8 (w/SS)	184.35
L35	Engine, 325-hp, 396-cid V-8 (w/SS)	63.20
L65	Engine, 250-hp, 350-cid V-8	21.10
L78	Engine, 375-hp, 396-cid V-8	316.00

Order #	Item Description	Sticker $
L89	Engine, 375-hp, V-8 (SS w/Alum Heads)	710.95
MB1	Transmission, Torque Drive	68.65
MC1	Transmission, Special 3-Speed	79.00
M11	Shift Lever, Floor Mounted	10.55
M20	Transmission, 4-Speed Wide Range	195.40
M21	Transmission, 4-Speed Close Ratio	195.40
M22	Transmission, 4-Speed Close Ratio HD	322.10
M35	Transmission, Powerglide (w/6-cyl)	163.70
M35	Transmission, Powerglide (w/V-8)	174.25
M40	Transmission, Turbo Hydra-Matic	190.10
NC8	Dual Exhaust System, Chambered	15.80
N10	Dual Exhaust System	30.55
N33	Steering Wheel, Comfortilt	45.30
N34	Steering Wheel, Wood-Grained	34.80
N40	Power Steering	94.80
N44	Steering, Quick Response	15.80
N65	Tire, Space Saver Spare	19.00
N95	Wheel Covers, Simulated Wire	73.75
N96	Wheel Covers, Mag-Style	73.75
PA2	Wheel Covers, Mag-Spoke	73.75
PK8	Tires, E78-14 Whitewall	32.10
PL5	Tires, F70-14 Lettered	63.05
PW7	Tires, F70-14 Whitewall	62.60
PW8	Tires, F70-14 Red Stripe	62.60
PY4	Tires, F70-14 Whitewall, F-Glass	88.60
PY4	Tires, F70-14 Whitewall, F-Glass (w/SS)	26.25
PY5	Tires, F70-14 Red Stripe, F-Glass	88.60
PY5	Tires, F70-14 Red Stripe, F-Glass (w/SS)	26.25
PO1	Wheel Covers, Bright Metal	21.10
PO6	Wheel Trim Rings	21.10
T60	Battery, Heavy-Duty	8.45
U15	Speed Warning Indicator	11.60
U17	Instrumentation, Special	94.80
U35	Clock, Electric	15.80
U16	Tachometer	52.70
U46	Light Monitoring System	26.35
U57	Stereo Tape System	133.80
U63	Radio, Pushbutton AM	61.10
U69	Radio, Pushbutton AM-FM	133.80
U73	Antenna, Rear Manual	9.50
U79	Radio, Pushbutton AM-FM Stereo	239.10
U80	Speaker, Rear Seat	13.20
VE3	Bumper, Special Body Color Front	42.15
V01	Radiator, Heavy-Duty	14.75
V31	Guard, Front Bumper	12.65
V32	Guard, Rear Bumper	12.65
V75	Liquid Tire Chain	23.20
ZJ7	Wheel Trim, Rally Wheels	35.85
ZJ9	Lighting, Auxiliary (Sp Cpe w/Z87)	11.10
ZJ9	Lighting, Auxiliary (Sp Cpe w/o Z87)	13.70
ZJ9	Lighting, Auxiliary (Conv w/Z87)	6.85
ZJ9	Lighting, Auxiliary (Conv w/o Z87)	9.50
ZK3	Belts, Custom Deluxe Seat and Shoulder	12.15
ZL2	Hood, Special Ducted	79.00
Z11	Special Indy 500 Convertible Accents	36.90
Z21	Style Trim Group	47.40
Z22	Rally Sport Package	131.65
Z23	Special Interior	17.95
Z27	Camaro Super Sport	295.95
Z28	Special Performance Package	458.15
Z87	Custom Interior	110.60
—	Two-Tone Paint	31.60

• Prices shown were introductory retail.

The Camaro had earned its wings by 1969, so badges proudly announced the Camaro identity and model designations. The "By Chevrolet" theme was seen on most Chevrolet product identification in 1969. Chevrolet photos.

Even with base trim, the 1969 Camaro convertible was an attractive automobile. The 327 badge on the front fender indicated this was a V-8 convertible and 15,866 of them were sold in 1969 compared to just 1,707 with six-cylinder engines. This particular car also had red-stripe tires and RPO PO1 full wheelcovers. Chevrolet photo.

—that elegance wasn't what the Camaro was all about. But my opinion is only that; an opinion. You may think the 1969 is the most beautiful first-generation Camaro, or even the most beautiful of all Camaros. If so, you aren't alone.

If the appearance of the 1969 Camaro suits you, there isn't a single disadvantage of ownership. Without question, it is the most mechanically refined of the first generation. Granted, there were more built than in either 1967 or 1968, but when the numbers exceed 200,000, who cares? It's the individual cars, the options, the condition that matter.

This Camaro finished the first generation of Camaros, yet it had a very individual identity. The car that followed it, the 1970, was fabulous, yet the popularity of the 1969 wasn't at all diminished. Part of that is because the 1970 hung around for over a decade. Its longevity is a tribute, but even the best of anything gets a little old after seeing it day in and day out for that long.

In the end, what followed 1969 didn't matter. The 1970 Camaro could have been one of the best cars of all time (which it was), or one of the worst. For the 1969, it just didn't matter. This car ended the Camaro's first generation, it ended the decade, and it created a fan club of unquestioned loyalty.

Which came first . . . glasses or headlamp covers?
Chevrolet photo.

Here are examples of right and wrong in the famous Camaro four-speed shift knob controversy. In a non-console application, the knob was a two-piece affair, black plastic with a metal base as shown. The shift pattern was etched into the knob. But with a console, the shift pattern was on the console itself and the knob was a plain, round, chrome-plated ball. The white knob shown was owner-added and incorrect for 1969. As a side note, all four-speed shifters used in 1969 Camaros were made by Hurst and "push down to reverse" wasn't required. Author photos.

When enthusiasts speak of documentation, they're referring to paperwork that confirms a Camaro is what it's represented to be. Examples include build sheets (coded guides used during assembly that owners often find tucked under the carpeting, dash, seats and so on), owner warranty plates, receipts, sales orders and, perhaps best of all, the original window stickers. Author photo.

When the factory installed rear spoilers on 1969 Camaros with Z-28-style wide stripes, the small portion of the trunk lip that extended below the back of the spoiler wasn't striped. The Z-28 shown with black stripes was factory-painted. Repainted Camaros, or dealer and customer spoiler installations, often have the trunk lip painted like the Z-28 shown with white stripes. Also, since the spoiler would have covered the Camaro name script, the script was moved forward on the rear deck lid, but its old mounting holes could still be found under the spoiler. Both Camaros photographed here had the RPO V32 rear bumper guard option which was standard with the Z-28. Similar guards were made for the front chrome bumper, but not for the body-colored "endura" front bumper option. Author photos.

Trunk space has always been at a premium in Camaros, but the inflatable-spare option (RPO N65) helped some. In 1969, 2,228 were sold. The Camaro pictured had the standard small wheel discs with optional trim rings (RPO P06 at $21.10). Chevrolet photo.

Trim identification tags for first-generation Camaros were located on the firewall, visible by lifting the hood. The tag shown was the later of two styles used by the Norwood, Ohio, Camaro assembly plant. Tags and codes for the California cars were different. Author photo.

Camaro seats for 1969 adjusted fore and aft with the lever along the side, and the back was released for entry to the rear seat by the lever behind the seat. A rake-angle adjustment for first-generation Camaros was never offered. Author photo.

Headlamps in 1969 Camaro Rally Sports were partially hidden by peephole-slit doors that slid out of the way by vacuum. And all 1969 Rally Sports came with headlight washers. These were little squirters, similar to windshield washers, that mounted above each headlamp. In order to work properly, the car had to be moving so that air pressure would flush the fluid across the lights. Like unused windshield washer lines, they tended to clog. Headlamp washers were available as a separate option for any Camaro in 1969, but only 116 non-Rally Sports got them. Author photos.

Some enthusiasts think the standard headlight treatment in 1969 Camaros made the car a little frog-eyed in front, but designers wanted a more aggressive appearance, and they got it. Super Sports without the RS option looked similar, but had a black-painted grille with an SS center emblem. Chevrolet photo.

1970 Model Production: 124,901

Sometimes a car just comes out right.

That's what happened with the 1970 Camaro. It was a designers' car, one done with emphasis on proportion. The first-generation Camaro was a designers' *and* engineers' car, compromised slightly because some of its components were to be shared later by the Chevy II. For 1970, there were no such compromises. This isn't to say that engineering took a back seat, just that appearance took precedence. The designers developed the proportions, and the engineers had to make it work. They did.

This car was new. Underneath, it was conceptually identical to the first-generation Camaro; that is, a subframe in front with a unitized body in the rear. Yet, virtually every piece under the new Camaro was new, as were the interior and the body.

What a body! With themes admittedly lifted from European exotics like the Jaguar and Aston Martin, the 1970 Camaro shape was magnificent. Where the original Camaro had been a Chevrolet project which Pontiac latched onto late for its Firebird rendition, the 1970 Camaro-Firebird was a joint design project for which both Chevrolet and Pontiac designers deserved credit.

The new Camaro could be criticized. It was slightly longer, lower and wider than the first generation, yet had a full cubic foot less cargo space. Rear seat room was tight in the first generation and even worse in the 1970. The doors of the new car were five inches longer than the earlier Camaros, which made rear seat entry easier. But the length of the doors made exit and entry in tight parking situations difficult. The doors' bulk, and the new, protective side-impact beams within them, made them heavy, to boot.

Pick, pick, pick. The things that counted in the Camaro market were looks, handling and power. In its May 1970 issue, *Car and Driver* magazine said of the 1970 Camaro Z-28, "It would be every bit as much at home on the narrow, twisting streets of Monte Carlo or in the courtyard of a villa overlooking the Mediterranean as it is on Interstate 80. It's a Camaro like none before." *Road & Track* concluded its own May 1970 article on the new Camaro by saying, "We'll have to say it's the best American car we've ever driven, and more importantly it's one of the most satisfying cars for all-around use we've ever driven."

Both magazines faulted the new Camaro's seat design (not enough lateral support, nonadjusting backrests), and *Road & Track* thought the brakes required too much pressure after hard use. But *Road & Track* later printed a retraction,

The editors of *Road & Track* magazine thought it was the best American car they'd ever driven. And a lot of people thought it was the best-looking car they'd ever seen. It was the 1970 Camaro. Chevrolet photo.

because Chevrolet demonstrated that the test car's brake pads hadn't been adequately burnished.

Chevrolet had a real winner with the 1970 Camaro, but there were those in the media who predicted it would soon fail. They weren't contending the Camaro wasn't a great car, only that it was too late. Chevrolet took its time getting into the ponycar market in the first place. Now here it was with the best entry yet, but just when the market was evaporating.

A successful decade later, this criticism looked pretty stupid. But in 1970, it didn't. Few were predicting the twin oil crises, but all knew the age of safety mandates and pollution-control requirements was upon the industry. Surely high-performance cars would suffer the most.

Of course, the Camaro not only survived, but the car introduced as the 1970 wound up the decade breaking its own sales records. The second-generation Camaro and its stablemate, the Firebird, lasted a full twelve model years, until the debut of the all-new and stunning 1982 Camaro model.

The 1970 Camaro might have led off the second generation, and a procession of success (with some dips), but much ended in 1970. The first of the second-generation Camaros was also the last of the pure fire-breathers. Camaros got better in some ways during the march into the eighties, but not in all ways. For now, let's concentrate on the 1970.

In the late sixties, the future for the convertible body style wasn't bright. Sales sagged, and manufacturers thought it possible that future federal rollover-crash-protection mandates would make it next to impossible to qualify convertibles. As it turned out, convertibles were exempted from the rollover requirements, but GM still decided to design the second-generation Camaro strictly as a two-door coupe. It rode on the same wheelbase (108 inches) as before and was lower, longer and wider than the first generation, but only slightly. The front bench seat, a low-volume option in 1967 and 1968, was dropped in 1969 and never returned.

Plenty of horsepower was available in 1970 models, but the choices narrowed. The base six-cylinder was the 250-cubic-inch-displacement, 155-horsepower engine instead of the previous year's 230-cubic-incher. This meant the base six

---

1970 Camaro

BASE ENGINE (SIX CYLINDER)
Type: . . . . Chevrolet ohv inline 6
Bore x stroke, inches: 3.875x3.53
Displacement, inches: 250
Compression ratio: 8.5:1
Horsepower: . . . . 155 @ 4200 rpm
Torque: . . . . .235 @ 1600 rpm
Distributor: .Single point breaker
Other engines offered: The base V-8 was 307-cid with 200-hp. Additional V-8 engines of 350-cid and 402-cid (called 396-cid) were available with power ratings from 250-hp to 375-hp.

CHASSIS AND DRIVETRAIN
Clutch: . . . . .Single dry-plate

Transmission: . . .Three speed manual standard. Four-speed manual, two-speed automatic and three-speed automatic optional.
Front suspension: . .Coil springs, tube-type shock absorbers
Rear suspension: . .Leaf springs, tube-type shock absorbers
Axle ratio: 2.73:1
Frame: . . . . .Box section front subframe, unibody rear
GENERAL
Wheelbase, inches: 108.0
Height, inches: 50.1
Width, inches: 74.4
Length, inches: 188.0
Brakes, standard: . . . . .Disc front, drum rear
Wheels: . . . . .Steel
Body material: . . . . .Steel
Tire size, base: E78-14
Fuel capacity, gallons: . . . . .19.0 (18.0 with RPO NA9)

The Rally Sport was much different in 1970, but then so was the entire Camaro line. The new RS package included various trim details, but the big news was in front. The Rally Sport featured small bumperettes, a protruding-snout grille framed in body-colored urethane, and European-style turn lamps set in the "catwalk" area between the headlights and grille. Stunning! Chevrolet photos.

Convertibles were no longer part of the Camaro act for 1970, so the base model choices were limited to six-cylinder and V-8 coupes. But the famous options of the first generation — Super Sport, Rally Sport (shown here) and, of course, Z-28 — were all back. Chevrolet photos.

The standard 1970 Camaro front styling was nice in its own right; it just suffered when compared to the Rally Sport. Prominent differences were the full-width front bumper, turn signals located under the bumper and a more conventional grille texture. Chevrolet photo.

RALLY SPORT

Beautiful? Yes. Practical? No. Actually, designers did manage to squeak a slightly reworked variation of this front end by the first vestiges of federal bumper standards in 1973. The Rally Sport package included trim items like side identification and color-keyed door handles. Rally Sport sales in 1970 were 27,136. Chevrolet photos.

The base 1970 interior shown had seating areas that looked like cloth but was textured vinyl. The Custom Interior could be cloth or vinyl. The short seatbacks with adjustable headrests were unique to 1970. A bench seat was not offered. Author photos.

One criticism of first-generation Camaros was the location of secondary instruments on the console. The second generation corrected that by including all instrumentation in the main instrument cluster, though some writers complained about the small size of the secondary gauges. All in all, the 1970's interior design was very well executed. Chevrolet photo.

was the only one in the Camaro lineup. The base V-8 continued to be the 307-cubic-inch engine with 200 horsepower.

Due to rule changes in the SCCA (Sports Car Club of America) Trans-Am racing series, the 302-cubic-inch engine was dropped as the Z-28 powerplant in the 1970 model and replaced by a 350-cubic-inch V-8 with 360 horsepower. As options, 250-horsepower and 300-horsepower versions of the 350-cubic-inch block were available. Two 396-cubic-inch (actually increased to 402 cubic inches in 1970, but not advertised that way) engines had ratings of 350 and 375 horsepower. The RPO LS6 and RPO LS7 versions of Chevrolet's huge 454-cubic-incher were scheduled for late introduction into the 1970 model, but Chevrolet changed its mind and the engines never made Camaro production.

A three-speed manual transmission was still standard with the base six-cylinder and base eight-cylinder Camaro coupes, but the heavy-duty three-speed manual and the do-it-yourself Torque Drive Powerglide semi-automatic were discontinued. All the V-8 engines came with the four-speed manual transmission at no cost. The three-speed Turbo Hydramatic was the optional automatic for all V-8 engines except the 375-horsepower, RPO L78 big-block, which could only be coupled with the four-speed manual.

All the familiar Camaro major option group names continued in 1970, but they didn't necessarily include the same things.

The Rally Sport was still a trim package, still easily recognized by a distinct front-end treatment. But previous Rally Sports had hidden headlights; the 1970 didn't. Instead, the Rally Sport of 1970 had a body-color urethane cap around a protruding central grille, small bumperettes at each side and very European-looking parking lamps positioned between the headlights and grille. Non-Rally Sports had a full-width bumper with standard-looking parking lamps under the

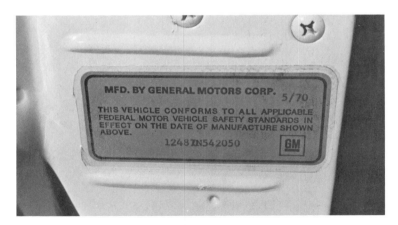

The driver's-side door jamb decal shows the date of manufacture and the Camaro's vehicle identification number. The actual VIN plate was attached to the top of the dash to be visible through the windshield, a change made in 1968 (1967's was on the door post) to conform to federal regulations. Author photo.

bumper. No doubt the non-Rally Sport bumper was more protective, but the styling of the Rally Sport front end was one of the best American design efforts ever. Some things need time to grow on you, but I loved the 1970 Rally Sport the first time I saw it and still do today.

The Rally Sport had special fender emblems, hidden windshield wipers, bright moldings for the roof gutter and back hood edge, different tail lamp bezels and color-coordinated outside door handles. The moldings, tail lamp bezels and door handles were available separately as the Style Trim option. Since designers didn't think the Rally Sport quite cut it with the base Camaro's dinky E78x14 tires, you were required to upgrade to at least the F78x14 size.

The Super Sport (SS) package was back also. Its $289.65 price included the 300-horsepower, 350-cubic-inch-displacement V-8 engine. RPO L34 and RPO L78 396 big-blocks with 350 and 375 horsepower, respectively, were available at extra cost in SS trim. All SS 1970 Camaros came with a four-speed manual transmission included, and the Turbo Hydramatic as optional with all but the 375-horsepower big-block. Both big-blocks had the RPO F41 special-performance suspension, which could be ordered separately in any other Camaro configuration.

If your 1970 Camaro was a Super Sport, it had power brakes, special ornamentation, hood insulation, 14x7-inch wheels, black-painted grille, hidden windshield wipers and SS emblems on the steering wheel, fenders, grille and rear deck lid.

The Z-28 package required ordering special instrumentation, four-speed manual or Turbo Hydramatic automatic transmission, power brakes and Positraction. As indicated earlier, the 1970 Z-28 came with a new, 350-cubic-inch, 360-horsepower engine, and it was a honey. The Z-28 package also had a heavy-duty radiator; bright engine accents; dual exhausts; black-painted grille; Z-28 emblems on the grille, front fenders and deck lid; rear bumper guards; special performance suspension (F41); heavy-duty front and rear springs; 15x7-inch wheels with bright lug nuts; special center caps and trim rings; hood insulation; F60x15 bias-belted tires with white letters; rear deck spoiler; and special paint stripes on the hood and rear deck. All this set you back $572.95, a small price to pay for a tremendous performance machine.

The 1970 Z-28 is a most desirable Camaro—perhaps *the* most desirable. It combined a thoroughly modern chassis with neck-snapping acceleration and handling to match. But in 1970, air conditioning and high-performance automobiles were still somewhat mutually exclusive. You couldn't order air with either the Z-28 or in an SS equipped with the 375-horsepower big-block.

The standard interior for the 1970 Camaro included all-vinyl bucket seats with small, adjustable headrests. An Accent Group option at $21.10 included additional instrument-cluster lighting and wood-grained accents on the instrument cluster and steering wheel. A center console was still optional, and if you ordered both console and the Accent Group, the simulated-wood treatment appeared on the console as well. The Custom Interior had everything the Accent Group did, plus upgraded seat vinyl (or cloth), glovebox light, luggage compartment mat and extra insulation. This cost $115.90.

Speaking of interior appointments, real instruments in place of warning lights still cost extra. The complaints about the console location of secondary instruments in the first Camaro generation had been heard, and all instruments in the 1970 car were right in front of the driver. The magazine people liked that,

The 1970 Camaro hood emblem was exclusive to the year. Author photo.

1970 Camaro Colors/Options

Color Code	Body Color
10	Classic White
14	Cortez Silver
17	Shadow Gray
25	Astro Blue
26	Mulsanne Blue
43	Citrus Green
45	Green Mist
48	Forest Green
51	Daytona Yellow
53	Camaro Gold
58	Autumn Gold
63	Desert Sand
65	Hugger Orange
67	Classic Copper
75	Cranberry Red

INTERIOR COLORS: Black, Bright Blue, Dark Green, Medium Saddle, Sandalwood, Black/Bright Blue, Black/Medium Green, Black/White

Order #	Item Description	Sticker $
12387	Base Camaro Sport Coupe, 6-cyl	2,749.00
12487	Base Camaro Sport Coupe, V-8	2,839.00
AK1	Belts, Color-Keyed Seat and Shoulder	12.15
AS4	Belts, Rear Shoulder	26.35
A01	Glass, Soft-Ray Tinted	37.95
B37	Mats, Color-Keyed Floor	11.60
B93	Moldings, Door Edge Guard	5.30
C08	Roof Cover, Vinyl	89.55
C24	Windshield Wiper, Hide-A-Way	19.00
C50	Defroster, Rear Window	26.35
C60	Air Conditioning, Four-Season	380.25
D34	Mirror, Visor Vanity	3.20
D35	Mirrors, Sport	26.35
D55	Console	59.00
D80	Spoiler, Rear Deck	32.65
F41	Suspension, Sport	30.55
G80	Axle, Positraction Rear	44.25
J50	Power Brakes	47.40

Order #	Item Description	Sticker $
L34	Engine, 350-hp, 396-cid V-8	152.75
L65	Engine, 250-hp, 396-cid V-8	31.60
L78	Engine, 375-hp, 396-cid V-8	385.50
M20	Transmission, 4-Speed Wide Ratio	205.95
M35	Transmission, Powerglide	174.25
M40	Transmission, Turbo Hydra-Matic	200.65
M40	Transmission, Turbo Hydra-Matic (w/L34)	221.80
M40	Transmission, Turbo Hydra-Matic (w/Z28)	290.40
NA9	Emission Control, California	36.90
N33	Steering Wheel, Comfortilt	45.30
N40	Power Steering	105.35
PL3	Tires, E78-14 Whitewall	26.05
PL4	Tires, F70-14 Lettered	65.35
PX6	Tires, F78-14 Whitewall	43.30
PY4	Tires, F70-14 Whitewall	65.70
P01	Wheel Trim, Bright Metal Wheel Covers	26.35
P02	Wheel Trim, Custom Covers	79.00
T60	Battery, heavy-Duty	15.80
U14	Instrumentation, Special	84.30
U35	Clock, Electric	15.80
U63	Radio, AM	61.10
U69	Radio, AM-FM	133.80
U80	Speaker, Rear Seat	14.75
VF3	Bumpers, Deluxe Front and Rear	36.90
V01	Radiator, Heavy-Duty	14.75
YD1	Axle, Trailering Ratio	12.65
ZJ7	Wheel Trim, Rally Wheels	42.15
ZJ9	Lighting, Auxiliary (w/o Z87)	13.70
ZJ9	Lighting, Auxiliary (w/Z87)	11.10
ZQ9	Axle, Performance Ratio	12.65
Z21	Style Trim	52.70
Z22	Rally Sport Package	168.55
Z23	Interior Accent Group	21.10
Z27	Camaro Super Sport	289.65
Z28	Special Performance Package	572.95
Z87	Custom Interior	115.90

• Prices shown were introductory retail.

but some felt the instruments were too small or could be blocked by the steering wheel. (Sometimes you just can't win!) On balance, the 1970 Camaro equipped with full instrumentation reflected a conscious effort on the part of designers to make the second-generation Camaro even more of a driver's car than the first.

Another first-generation Camaro criticism had been the interior noise level. Engineers went to work on noise isolation in the second generation. The most significant result was a double-roof section, with the normal outer skin and a perforated steel liner and thin mylar blanket added. According to Michael Lamm's *The Camaro Book from A Through Z-28,* this new roof design absorbed eighty-four percent of the resonance present inside the car, compared with twenty-eight percent for the 1969 Camaro.

Much additional noise reduction was accomplished with the seat-of-the-pants, sweat-of-the-brow method, where engineers sought to find and seal every joint or body gap where noise could enter.

I guessed in the previous chapter that if Camaro enthusiasts voted on the all-around best Camaro, the 1969 would be in the running. So would the 1970. In fact, I think these two years would run neck-and-neck for the top spot, although prices of 1970 models have been considerably lower so far.

We've already discussed the 1969's position as the last and most refined of the first generation, so at first thought it might seem that the 1970 would also have benefited from a few more years of development and refinement. In some ways this happened, but the 1970 Camaro's big virtue was power. It was the first year of a long string of second-generation Camaros, but it was also the last year for ultra-high-compression engines in GM products.

General Motors reduced compression ratios voluntarily in 1971, so that oil companies could begin phasing-in lower-octane, unleaded fuels, in order that no-lead fuel would be widely available by 1975. That's when manufacturers would equip most cars with catalytic converters, which couldn't tolerate lead. The pollution-control factors and safety requirements ganged up on high-performance cars by causing weights to increase and power outputs to go down. General Motors played the good corporate citizen and led the way in 1971 by detuning its high-output engines; most other domestics followed in 1972.

But keep the proper perspective on this high-compression consideration. There is no question that the high-performance cars built before compression ratios were dropped are highly collectible. The brute power of these cars—cars that could be purchased by virtually anyone who could walk into their local dealer and sign the loan application—is really astonishing by today's standards. But if you wish to use one of these cars for daily transportation today, you'll pay a price. Pump fuel, other than at your local airport, may simply not be available with adequately high octane. There is a handful of stations that do blend their own high-octane concoctions, and you can mix-in octane boosters yourself at every fill-up. Either way, you can add at least fifty percent to what you'd normally expect to pay for fuel. Another option is to retard timing slightly, then blend a mixture of two-thirds unleaded premium with one-third leaded regular. Of course, you'll sacrifice some of the engine's power potential. You might find that your high-compression engine runs fine on the best unleaded available. Even so, you should mix in some leaded fuel, because the lead helps prevent burned valves in pre-catalytic-converter engines.

And not all Camaro engines lost power between 1970 and 1971; we're talking about the high-performance engines. The base six had a compression ratio of

This COPO 9796 rear spoiler was one of two styles used in 1970. The other (RPO D80), smaller and one piece, resembled the 1969 style. The three-piece COPO style looked more aggressive and it became part of a revised RPO D80 front and rear spoiler option package for later Camaro model years. Author photo.

Here's a closeup view of the 1970 Z-28 rear emblem. The lock tumbler below it released the trunk. The fuel filler was behind the hinged license plate holder. Author photo.

The standard wheel for a 1970 Z-28 was this 15x7-inch mag style with trim rings and bright lug nuts. The lug nuts in this photo aren't original, but the F60-15/B bias-belted white-letter tire is. Author photo.

Rally Sports and Z-28's went together in 1970 like peanut butter and jelly, but most Rally Sports weren't Z's, and many Z-28's had standard front ends like this one. On Rally Sports, the Z-28 emblem went into the lower portion of the grille, but with full-width bumper models, it was placed higher in the grille to be visible over the bumper. Author photo.

8.5:1 in 1970, and that's where it stayed in 1971. The base V-8 did drop from 9.0:1 to 8.5:1, but its horsepower rating remained at 200. So, even though the 1970 does have special status as a collector car, there isn't any overwhelming logic to selecting it over the following year if you're after a low-horsepower car. And the high-performance engines of the following years, while less powerful than their earlier counterparts, do run agreeably on today's fuels.

Still, there's no question the 1970 Camaro is held in high esteem by Camaro enthusiasts. You can find things about later years that make them desirable in their own right (I'll point out many to you), yet there are a good number of Camaro enthusiasts whose interest starts with 1967 models and ends with the 1970. Period.

The 1970 is a difficult car to fault. For obvious reasons, the Z-28 is the strongest collector car, but the Super Sports are also highly desirable. The Rally Sport front end was incredibly well styled, and I wouldn't have a 1970 any other way. But you'd rule out some fine examples if you took this attitude.

I mentioned earlier that air conditioning could not be ordered with the Z-28 option, nor in the SS396 with 375 horsepower. That's a little out of sync with today's belief that you don't have to be uncomfortable to enjoy a high-performance car. So if you plan to buy a 1970 Camaro to use, you may wish to look at other engine choices.

Another shortcoming of the 1970 Camaro (really, of most Camaros in the first and second generations) was the seating. The legs-out driving position of Camaros required better-than-average seats, but Camaro seats were average at best. Some people aren't troubled by the lack of support and adjustability, but I've always been bothered. If the car isn't driven much, it doesn't matter. But if it is, the solution might be an aftermarket seat like the Recaro.

About the only other negative point I can think of for 1970 was the lack of one of my favorite exterior colors: black. It was available the previous three years, and it was back on the list for 1971.

Some of the more sedate first-generation Camaros should emerge as quite desirable collector cars, but the same probably isn't true of 1970. Chevrolet built 1,936,869 second-generation Camaros over a twelve-year period. Unless you have your own island, you can't walk outside without seeing a second-generation Camaro pass by within minutes. Plain-Jane second-generation Camaros, the 1970 included, are just nice used cars so far. If you're going to part with serious funds, or devote considerable hours to a 1970 Camaro restoration, pick one that'll raise your blood pressure when you walk into the garage.

1971 Model Production: 114,630

Chevrolet didn't make major changes in the 1971 Camaro. After all, the 1970 model was brand new, and its late introduction gave it little more than half a normal sales year.

The two models looked similar, but the 1971 had features that set it apart. The most apparent visual change was in the interior. The 1970 Camaro had low-back front bucket seats with adjustable headrests. The 1971's were high-back types adapted from the Vega. Most people thought the new seats were more comfortable, even though the back angle was still quite upright. (One magazine writer compared it to sitting in an unfolded lawn chair.) Chevrolet finally did add an optional seatback adjustment for the 1971 Camaro, but it was available only for the driver's side and had only two positions. This was RPO AN6 at $19.

Other differences were minor. Nameplates were redesigned. Of the fifteen exterior colors for 1971, twelve were new and three were carried over. Five vinyl-top colors could be selected, two more than for the 1970. Interior knobs were redone with soft surfaces for added safety when impacted. A new, cushioned steering wheel was also added for safety reasons.

Windshield glass was thinner. The front side-marker lights flashed with the turn signals. The base and optional axles were beefed-up. A front air dam was added to the RPO D80 spoiler option. The D80 was a taller spoiler than the standard Z-28 spoiler, but it could be added to the Z-28. Either way, the Z-28 came with a front spoiler.

The big news for 1971 was under the hood. This was the year that GM lowered compression ratios in its high-compression engines. It was also the year that GM decided to phase-in a new method of rating horsepower. Through the 1970 models, GM's ratings were gross; that is, the amount of power the engine alone produced. In 1972, the ratings became net, which was the power actually delivered to the driving wheels. Because of accessory and driveline power losses, net ratings were lower. Nineteen seventy-one was the transition year, so GM listed both gross and net power ratings. All of this was intended to pacify insurance people and government types who determined that the horsepower race had gotten out of hand.

Nineteen seventy-one was a tough sales year for Camaro because General Motors had jumped the gun in detuning its high-performance engines; the competition held off until 1972. Just what this meant is illustrated by the Z-28. In 1970, its 350-cubic-inch engine developed 360 horsepower with an 11.0:1 compression ratio. With its compression ratio dropped to 9.0:1 in 1971, horsepower

The 1971 Camaro looked practically the same as 1970. There was no point in tampering with a good thing; the 1970 Camaro model year was a short one because of its late introduction, anyway. Chevrolet photo.

The front emblem was the same for all 1971 Camaros, but it differed in detail from the 1970. Author photo.

The easiest way to distinguish a 1971 model from the 1970 was by checking the seats. The 1971 had high-back-style seats; the 1970 backs were low with separate headrests. When the Rally Sport was combined with the Super Sport as shown, the grille didn't carry SS identification. This car had RPO PL4 white-letter tires mounted on RPO ZJ7 Rally wheels. Chevrolet photo.

decreased to 330. The 360- and 330-horsepower figures were equivalent because they were both gross. The Camaro's 1971 Z-28 net rating was 275 horsepower.

A thirty-horsepower loss may not seem like the end of the world, and you wouldn't miss it driving to the hardware store on Saturday morning. But for any kind of competition where fractions of a second are the margin between victory and defeat, those thirty missing horses could be devastating.

Chevrolet saw this coming and tentatively planned to open the 350-cubic-inch engine up to 400 cubes for the 1971 Z-28. Even with the loss in compression, Chevrolet thought the extra fifty inches would keep the Z-28 in the same performance ballpark. Chevrolet built prototypes of the small-block 400, and even told journalists at the 1971 long-lead press preview in the summer of 1970 that the 400 was coming. But higher management within General Motors wanted no part of it, and the engine was never put into Camaros.

Here's what the rest of the engine situation looked like in 1971 Camaros: The base six was still the 250-cubic-inch-displacement engine, and its compression ratio stayed unchanged at 8.5:1. It carried a gross rating of 145 horsepower and a net rating of 110 horsepower. The base V-8 was the 307-cubic-inch engine with 200 horsepower gross, and 140 horsepower net. The gross rating was the same as the previous year, even though compression did drop from 9.0:1 to 8.5:1.

Along with the Z-28's 330-horsepower, 350-cubic-inch-displacement engine, there were two other 350-cubic-inch engines. The RPO L65 had 245 horsepower

The 1970 and 1971 models were so similar in appearance, Chevrolet stuck a 1971 license plate on this 1970 for sales promotion, and few knew the difference. But the low-back seats betray this as a 1970. Both years did display the SS emblem in the grille of non-Rally Sports. The fancy wheelcovers were RPO PO2 and cost $84.30. In 1971, only 1,809 sets of the wire covers were sold, compared to 3,532 in 1970. Chevrolet photo.

gross and 165 horsepower net. The RPO L48 had 270 horsepower gross and 210 net. Compression ratios of both engines dropped to 8.5:1. Only one big-block 396 could be ordered. It was the RPO LS3 with 8.5:1 compression, 300 horsepower gross and 260 horsepower net.

The major options continued from 1970 with just minor changes. The RPO Z78 Custom Interior included cloth seats with vinyl trim instead of a choice between cloth or vinyl as before. Air conditioning was available on all models except the Z-28.

The 1971 model lost two months' production to a United Auto Workers (UAW) strike from September 14, 1970, through November 22, 1970; the total Camaro production for the year was 114,630. That was quite low, as annual production of each of the three first-generation Camaros was well over 200,000, and even the half-year 1970 model reached 124,901. The strike did put an early dent into sales, but it wasn't responsible for the poor showing by year's end.

1971 Camaro Colors/Options

Color Code	Body Color
11	White
13	Steel Silver
19	Tuxedo Black
24	Medium Blue
26	Bright Blue
42	Palm Green
43	Lime Green
49	Dark Green
52	Bright Yellow
53	Bright Yellow (Metallic)
61	Light Sandalwood
62	Burnt Orange
67	Sienna
75	Red
78	Dark Rosewood

INTERIOR COLORS: Black, Dark Blue, Dark Jade, Saddle, Sandalwood, Black/Blue, Black/Jade, Black/Saddle, Black/White

Order #	Item Description	Sticker $
12387	Base Camaro Sport Coupe, 6-cyl	2,758.00
12487	Base Camaro Sport Coupe, V-8	2,848.00
AK1	Belts, Color-Keyed Seat and Shoulder	15.30
AN6	Seat Back, Adjustable	19.00
AS4	Belts, Rear Shoulder	26.35
A01	Glass, Soft-Ray Tinted	40.05
B37	Mats, Color-Keyed Floor	12.65
B93	Moldings, Door Edge Guard	6.35
C08	Roof Cover, Vinyl	89.55
C24	Windshield Wipers, Hide-A-Way	21.10
C50	Defroster, Rear Window	31.60
C60	Air Conditioning, Four-Season	402.35
D34	Mirror, Visor Vanity	3.20
D35	Mirror, Sport	15.80
D55	Console	59.00
D80	Spoilers, Front and Rear	79.00
F41	Suspension, Sport	30.55
G80	Axle, Positraction Rear	44.25
J50	Power Brakes	47.30
LS3	Engine, 300-hp, 396-cid V-8	99.05

Order #	Item Description	Sticker $
L65	Engine, 245-hp, 350-cid V-8	26.35
M20	Transmission, 4-Speed Wide Ratio	205.95
M21	Transmission, 4-Speed Close Ratio	205.95
M22	Transmission, 4-Speed Close Ratio HD	237.60
M35	Transmission, Powerglide (w/6-cyl)	179.55
M35	Transmission, Powerglide (w/V-8)	190.10
M40	Transmission, Turbo Hydra-Matic	216.50
M40	Transmission, Turbo Hydra-Matic (w/LS3)	237.60
M40	Transmission, Turbo Hydra-Matic (w/Z28)	306.25
NK2	Steering Wheel, Custom	15.80
NK4	Steering Wheel, Sport	15.80
N33	Steering Wheel, Comfortilt	45.30
N40	Power Steering	110.60
PL3	Tires, E78-14 Whitewall	26.05
PL4	Tires, F70-14 Lettered	81.50
PY4	Tires, F70-14 Whitewall	68.05
PO1	Wheel Trim, Bright Metal Wheel Covers	26.35
PO2	Wheel Trim, Custom Covers	84.30
T60	Battery, Heavy-Duty	15.80
U14	Instrumentation, Special	84.30
U35	Clock, Electric	16.90
U63	Radio, AM	66.40
U69	Radio, AM-FM	139.05
U80	Speaker, Rear Seat	15.80
VF3	Bumpers, Deluxe Front and Rear	36.90
V01	Radiator, Heavy-Duty	14.75
YD1	Axle, Trailering Ratio	12.65
ZJ7	Wheel Trim, Rally Wheels	45.30
ZJ9	Lighting, Auxiliary (w/o Z87)	18.45
ZJ9	Lighting, Auxiliary (w/Z87)	15.80
ZQ9	Axle, Performance Ratio	12.65
Z21	Style Trim	57.95
Z22	Rally Sport Package	179.05
Z23	Interior Accent Group	21.10
Z27	Camaro Super Sport	313.90
Z28	Special Performance Package	786.75
Z87	Custom Interior	115.90

• Prices shown were introductory retail.

Door panels in 1971 were like the previous year. This one had the standard outside rearview mirror so there was no remote-control lever. Power windows weren't a second-generation option until 1973. The knob to the left of the heater and air-conditioning controls opened and closed the air vent. Author photo.

This was the 1971 standard interior with the RPO Z23 Accent Group, which included wood-graining for the instrument area and steering wheel, but nowhere else. Notice that the stirrup selector handle for an automatic with console was still being used. The stirrup was beautiful in appearance and worked great, but there were safety concerns about its design. It was gone in 1973. Author photo.

Chevrolet did another breakaway display for its 1971 Camaro, an SS-RS model. The front section showed that Chevrolet engineers continued to use a front subframe design concept quite similar to the first generation. Chevrolet photo.

Throughout most of 1971, dealers had more Camaros than they could sell, and Chevrolet had to hustle to unload even the reduced quantities built.

All this paints a ho-hum picture for the 1971 Camaro. It looks like a year with nothing superior (save the seats) over the previous model, and a few disadvantages, the lower-compression engines being most obvious.

Compared to its own 1970 model, the 1971 Camaro didn't improve significantly, but by any other measure it was still an excellent automobile. In fact, *Road & Track* selected the 1971 Camaro SS350 as one of the world's ten best cars in its August 1971 issue. The Camaro was judged the best sedan in the $4,000-$6,000 price range. *Road & Track* said, "The Chevrolet Camaro proves that Detroit can build a good, esthetically pleasing road car for a reasonable price. Its classification as a sedan is somewhat equivocal; we could have easily

Early second-generation Camaro rear end design was clean, too clean for those who preferred the spoiler addition. The standard outside rear-view mirror was the chrome model pictured. Other than the emblem, the 1971 standard front end duplicated the 1970's. Author photos.

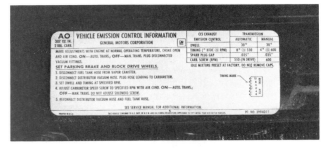

The VIN plate was mounted on the dash and was visible
through the windshield. The first five digits indicated the
model type (12487 was a V-8 coupe), the sixth digit was the
year (1 meant 1971), the N stood for the Norwood assembly
plant and the remaining numbers increased one digit with
each car produced. This was Camaro number 8,745 built at
Norwood in 1971. The emission control information label
was placed on top of the radiator. Author photos.

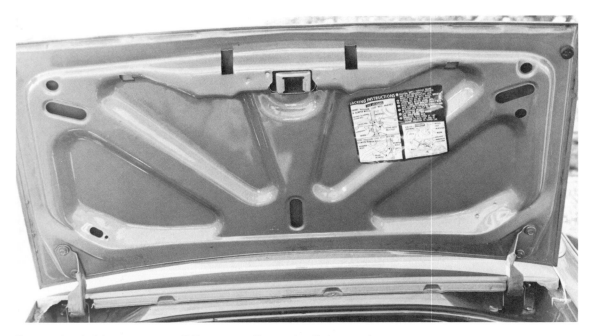

Camaro trunk lids were so small there weren't any nice flat areas for
labels, so they usually wrapped over the ridges like this jacking instructions label. Author photo.

called it a Sports GT, but whatever the category, it is an outstanding car. Chevrolet engineers seriously tried to incorporate in it lessons learned from European GT's and in doing so gave it adequate suspension, standard front disc brakes, a good driving position and wide wheels and tires. Meanwhile, the stylists were giving it an astonishingly beautiful body, albeit an overlarge and not particularly space-efficient one. But for less than $5,000 one can buy a Camaro 350SS and it's one great hunk of car for that money."

Not only did the experts agree on the Camaro's value, but consumers—at least those in the enthusiast category—did as well. In *Car and Driver's* Readers' Poll for 1971, the Camaro easily won the voting for the ponycar class, getting twice as many votes as the Mustang.

Despite these accolades, the 1971 Camaro simply doesn't have the collector appeal of the 1970. What we've got here is a situation that reminds me of the value difference between the 1963 and 1964 Corvette coupes. The owner of a 1964 can cite you several little improvements his car has over the 1963. But the 1963 was the start of the Sting Ray series, and it had that split rear window. The split gives the 1963 Corvette coupe collector magic, and it's worth several thousand dollars more.

Similarly, the 1971 Camaro is almost a duplicate of the 1970 car, but there's a certain magic to the 1970's status as the first of the series, and the last of the high-compression era. All things being equal, you can expect to pay less for a 1971, and to sell it for less later.

But a nicely optioned 1971 in beautiful condition is not a car to be ignored. Because its halo is a little smaller than the 1970's, you just might be able to buy one for less than it's worth. When *Road & Track* picked it as one of the world's ten best, it was the *only* U.S.-built car on the list. So it certainly has credentials.

1971 Camaro
BASE ENGINE (SIX CYLINDER)
Type: . . . . Chevrolet ohv inline 6
Bore x stroke, inches: 3.875x3.53
Displacement, inches: 250
Compression ratio: 8.5:1
Horsepower: . . 145 @ 4200 rpm gross, 110 @ 3800 rpm net
Torque: . . . . . . 230 @ 1600 rpm gross, 185 @ 1600 rpm net
Distributor: . . . . Single point breaker
Other engines offered: The base V-8 was 307-cid with 200-hp gross, 140-hp net. Additional V-8 engines of 350-cid and 402-cid (called 396-cid) were available with power ratings from 245-hp gross (165-hp net) to 330-hp gross (275-hp net).
CHASSIS AND DRIVETRAIN
Clutch: . . . . Single dry-plate

Transmission: . . . Three speed manual standard. Four-speed manual, two-speed automatic and three-speed automatic optional.
Front suspension: . . Coil springs, tube-type shock absorbers
Rear suspension: . . Leaf springs, tube-type shock absorbers
Axle ratio: 3.08:1
Frame: . . . . Box section front subframe, unibody rear
GENERAL
Wheelbase, inches: 108.0
Height, inches: 50.5
Width, inches: 74.4
Length, inches: 188.0
Brakes, standard: . . . . Disc front, drum rear
Wheels: . . . . Steel
Body material: . . . . Steel
Tire size, base: E78-14
Fuel capacity, gallons: 17.0

CHAPTER 6
1972 Camaro

★★★ SS350
★★★★ SS396
★★★★ Z-28

• Add ★ for Rally Sport

1972 Model Production: 68,651

All great cars go through periods of uncertainty. For the Camaro, one such period came in 1972.

President Richard Nixon froze prices nationwide in 1972, and federal excise taxes were rolled back seven percent on U.S. automobiles, including the Camaro. This gave the floundering auto industry a shot of adrenaline, but Camaros and Firebirds got bushwhacked by the United Auto Workers. The UAW took out the Norwood, Ohio, assembly plant (the only one building Camaros and Firebirds at the time) for 117 days, starting on April 7, 1972. When the strike was over, so was the production model year; 1,100 partially assembled Camaros had to be scrapped because it was too expensive to bring them into compliance with tougher 1973 safety and emission requirements.

The 1972 Camaro was the lowest-volume Camaro ever, with just 68,651 sold. The strike wasn't the Camaro's fault, but it and the Camaro's generally slow sales rate, even when cars were available, caused some within the executive ranks of General Motors to wonder if the time hadn't come to get rid of the Camaro altogether.

The American auto industry was entering a difficult decade. Each year, government safety and emission regulations became more stringent, and it was a battle for manufacturers just to keep all of their car lines legal. Engine choices dwindled, because it wasn't feasible to certify numerous engines for each car line. It certainly looked like an appropriate time to eliminate slow-selling models and concentrate on the higher-volume moneymakers.

The Camaro and Firebird were strong candidates for the scrap heap. They had been conceived as personal sporty cars with emphasis on style, handling and performance, but not efficiency. If getting from point A to point B was the only mission, other cars could move more people at less cost.

Car-enthusiast managers within Chevrolet and Pontiac felt their Camaro and Firebird were too good to let go. The market was evaporating, but so was the competition. If the market came back, they argued, Chevrolet and Pontiac would be superbly positioned. The Camaro and Firebird were costly to develop, but they were great cars, and they both had strong—though limited in numbers—customer loyalty.

One reason those in favor of dropping the Camaro picked 1972 was that the following year would bring tough, new front bumper regulations. It was feared that the whole Camaro front end would have to be expensively redesigned. But engineers finagled ways to get the Camaro certified at much less cost than original-

The Camaro for 1972 continued with the good looks introduced in 1970. The grille of non-Rally Sports like the one shown featured a coarser mesh. If this car had been a Super Sport, the rear panel would have been painted black. Chevrolet photos.

The Rally Sport for 1972 looked like those of the previous two years. This one had the optional front and rear spoiler package. It was RPO D80 and cost $77. The rear spoiler was a nicely fitted and finished, rigid plastic assembly of three pieces, the center one lifting with the trunk lid. But the front air dam, shipped loose from the factory for dealer installation, was a flexible affair that always looked distorted. Sales of the spoiler package in 1971 were 5,954. Chevrolet photos.

The 1972 Camaro trunk floor was splatter-painted. A mat came with the Custom Interior, but otherwise it looked just as you see it here. The funny black shape extending from under the spare tire was a cover for the jack. Author photo.

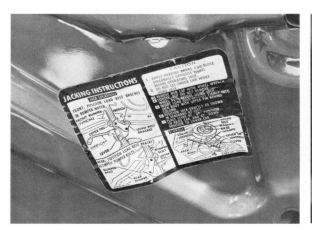

Jacking instruction and Positraction warning labels were placed on the inner trunk surface, but precise locations varied. This 1972 had the jacking label on the driver's side by the trunk light, and the Positraction label on the opposite side toward the front of the lid. Since this Camaro had the Custom Interior, it was treated to a trunk mat. The plastic cones protected the taillight apparatus from objects sliding in the trunk. Author photos.

ly thought. And they managed to do it with minimal change to the car's appearance. This feat was the single most important factor in pulling the Camaro through those hard times.

In appearance, the 1972 Camaro was a dead ringer for the 1971 model. If the 1972 was a standard model (non-Rally Sport), its grille did have a coarser mesh. The Rally Sport was the same as before.

Engine choices didn't change a bit, but horsepower ratings dropped for four of the six engines due to emissions tinkering. General Motors rated 1972 engines by net output only. Comparing the net power ratings of 1972 and 1971 Camaros, the base 307-cubic-inch-displacement V-8 dropped from 140 to 130 horsepower, the optional RPO L48 350-cubic-inch V-8 from 210 to 200 horsepower, and the optional RPO LS3 396-cubic-inch big-block from 260 to 240 horsepower. The once-thundering 350-cubic-inch Z-28 motor still had solid lifters (the last year for solids), but output went from 275 to 255 horsepower. The big-block couldn't be ordered by California residents because its volume was too low to justify the separate California emission certification.

Transmissions didn't change, but the four-speed manual got a new shifter with a push-down reverse lockout.

The interior option packages were the same as in 1971, but 1972 Camaros did get a new door trim panel with a coin holder and map pockets in the armrest. Vinyl roofs on 1972 Camaros adopted the "wet" look, a fad that, fortunately, passed as quickly as it came.

Option lists for all cars, Camaros included, shrank as each year of the seventies ticked off, with manufacturers trying to rein-in model and accessory proliferation. When scores of options are available, the ad people say that's wonderful because customers can tailor cars just the way they want them. When it goes the

The 1972 Z-28 engine looked impressive with its dual-snorkel air cleaner with chromed top, and finned aluminum valve covers. In its 1972 form, it developed 255 horsepower. Author photo.

The base V-8 engine for 1972 was the L69 which developed 165 horsepower. The air cleaner and valve covers were painted, and the carburetor was a two-barrel. Author photo.

The steering wheel was different (RPO NK4 in 1971 and 1972); otherwise, the instrument panel for 1972 looked like the earlier second-generation models. The door trim panels were new, though, featuring deep map pockets and a little doodad tray just forward of the armrest. The Custom Interior version in this photo had simulated wood inlays. Shoulder belts were independent from the lap belts. Author photos.

The gorgeous "catwalk" turn-signal light for Rally Sports in 1972 was the same as in the previous two years. In fact, this 1972 lens had a 1970 code cast-in. The lens was clear, the bulb amber. Author photo.

Hide-A-Way Windshield Wipers (RPO C24) was a separate option from 1970 through 1976 in Camaros (also included in specific groups during these years and later). With this option, the wipers hid under the hood lip when not in use; without it, they were visible on the windshield. The hidden wiper option also included an "articulated" left-hand blade, a double-arm design that gave the blade better glass contact. It seems like a minor point, but enthusiasts aware of the difference prefer the cleaner look of the hidden style. Author photos.

1972 Camaro

BASE ENGINE (SIX CYLINDER)

Type: . . . . .Chevrolet ohv inline 6
Bore x stroke, inches: .3.875x3.53
Displacement, inches: 250
Compression ratio: 8.5:1
Horsepower: . . . . .110 @ 3800 rpm (net)
Torque: . . . . .185 @ 1600 rpm (net)
Distributor: .Single point breaker
Other engines offered: . .The base V-8 was 307-cid with 130-hp net. Additional V-8 engines of 350-cid and 402-cid (called 396-cid) were available with power ratings from 165-hp to 255-hp net.

CHASSIS AND DRIVETRAIN

Clutch: . . . . .Single dry-plate

Transmission: . . .Three speed manual standard. Four-speed manual, two-speed automatic and three-speed automatic optional.
Front suspension: . .Coil springs, tube-type shock absorbers
Rear suspension: . .Leaf springs, tube-type shock absorbers
Axle ratio: 3.08:1
Frame: . . . . .Box section front subframe, unibody rear

GENERAL

Wheelbase, inches: 108.0
Height, inches: 50.5
Width, inches: 74.4
Length, inches: 188.0
Brakes, standard: . . . . .Disc front, drum rear
Wheels: . . . . .Steel
Body material: . . . . .Steel
Tire size, base: E78-14
Fuel capacity, gallons: 18.0

other way, that's said to be wonderful too, because the people who design the cars can group the equipment intelligently. That way cars on showroom floors, where most are bought, wind up with more sensible equipment mixes. Additionally, Chevrolet started using advertising to suggest how Camaro options could be grouped to provide rather different types of automobiles, depending on customer need or preference.

Road & Track, usually somewhat biased toward European cars (which came with short option lists), thought the move toward "factory equipped" U.S. cars was a good thing and decided to take Chevrolet's hint. In its April 1972 issue, *Road & Track* tested three Camaros equipped for three different purposes: First was *The Budget GT,* a base V-8 with four-speed manual transmission, sports suspension (RPO F41), full instrumentation (RPO U14), power brakes, power steering and Positraction. Second was *The Luxury GT,* another base V-8, but with automatic transmission, power steering and brakes, air conditioning, clock and rear window defroster (RPO ZQ2), and the RPO Z87 Custom Interior. The third

1972 Camaro Colors/Options

Color Code	Body Color
11	Antique White
14	Pewter Silver
24	Ascot Blue
26	Mulsanne Blue
36	Spring Green
43	Gulf Green
48	Sequoia Green
50	Covert Tan
53	Placer Gold
56	Cream Yellow
57	Golden Brown
63	Mohave Gold
65	Flame Orange
68	Midnight Bronze
75	Cranberry Red

INTERIOR COLORS: Black, Dark Blue, Light Covert, Dark Green, Medium Tan, White

Order #	Item Description	Sticker $
12387	Base Camaro Sport Coupe, 6-cyl	2,729.70
12487	Base Camaro Sport Coupe, V-8	2,819.70
AK1	Belts, Color-Keyed Seat and Shoulder	14.50
AN6	Seat Back, Adjustable	18.00
A01	Glass, Soft-Ray Tinted	39.00
B37	Mats, Color-Keyed Floor	12.00
B93	Moldings, Door Edge Guard	6.00
C08	Roof Cover, Vinyl	87.00
C24	Windshield Wipers, Hide-A-Way	21.00
C50	Defogger, Rear Window	31.00
C60	Air Conditioning, Four-Season	397.00
D34	Mirror, Visor Vanity	3.00
D35	Mirror, Sport	15.00
D55	Console	57.00
D80	Spoilers, Front and Rear	77.00
F41	Suspension, Sport	30.00
G80	Axle, Positraction Rear	45.00
J50	Power Brakes	46.00
LS3	Engine, 240-hp, 396-cid V-8	96.00
L65	Engine, 165-hp, 350-cid V-8	26.00

Order #	Item Description	Sticker $
M20	Transmission, 4-Speed Wide Ratio	200.00
M21	Transmission, 4-Speed Close Ratio	200.00
M22	Transmission, 4-Speed Close Ratio HD	231.00
M35	Transmission, Powerglide (w/6-cyl)	174.00
M35	Transmission, Powerglide (w/V-8)	185.00
M40	Transmission, Turbo Hydra-Matic	210.00
M40	Transmission, Turbo Hydra-Matic (w/LS3)	231.00
M40	Transmission, Turbo Hydra-Matic (w/Z28)	297.00
NK4	Steering Wheel, Sport	15.00
N33	Steering Wheel, Comfortilt	44.00
N40	Power Steering	130.00
PL3	Tires, E78-14 Whitewall	28.00
PL4	Tires, F70-14 Lettered	82.85
PY4	Tires, F70-14 Whitewall	69.85
P01	Wheel Trim, Bright Metal Wheel Covers	26.00
P02	Wheel Trim, Custom Covers	82.00
T60	Battery, Heavy-Duty	15.00
U14	Instrumentation, Special	82.00
U35	Clock, Electric	16.00
U63	Radio, AM	65.00
U69	Radio, AM-FM	135.00
U80	Speaker, Rear Seat	15.00
VF3	Bumpers, Deluxe Front and Rear	36.00
V01	Radiator, Heavy-Duty	14.00
YD1	Axle, Trailering Ratio	12.00
YF5	Emission Test, California	15.00
ZJ7	Wheel Trim, Rally Wheels	44.00
ZJ9	Lighting, Auxiliary (w/o Z87)	17.50
ZJ9	Lighting, Auxiliary (w/Z87)	15.00
ZQ9	Axle, Performance Ratio	12.00
Z21	Style Trim	56.00
Z22	Rally Sport Package	118.00
Z23	Interior Accent Group	21.00
Z27	Camaro Super Sport	306.35
Z28	Special Performance Package	769.15
Z87	Custom Interior	113.00

• Prices shown were lower than 1972 model introductory prices due to the repeal of federal excise taxes.

Here's one to watch. Although detuned a bit, only 2,575 Z-28 Camaros were built in 1972, and this one's a Rally Sport to boot. The 1972 was the last second-generation Z-28 with solid valve lifters and aluminum intake manifold. But for even more scarcity, search out a 1972 SS396. It was the last year for big-blocks in Camaros, and Chevrolet dealers delivered just 970. Author photos.

to be tested was *The Performance GT,* a Z-28 with Turbo Hydramatic transmission and a few concessions to luxury like the Custom Interior and tilt steering wheel.

Road & Track found all three cars performed their missions well and refused to pick a favorite. The reader got the impression it wasn't the Z-28, not because the Z-28 wasn't a fine car; just that the writers didn't like what it had become, compared to what it had been.

Road & Track thought it good that Chevrolet had added an optional back rake adjustment to the seats, but was displeased that it had only two settings, four degrees apart. "It's a good idea, insufficiently executed." It liked the extra sound insulation, but didn't like the fake wood that came with it as part of the Custom Interior option. The article was generally upbeat, concluding, "The budget car doesn't lack luxury, the performance car doesn't lack comfort, and the luxury car doesn't lack performance."

Evaluation of a 1972 Camaro for purchase today is a rehash of 1971. On its own, the 1972 was a fine car. The Rally Sport still looked like the 1970 edition, and that was hard to beat. Four of the six engines were weaker than the previous year's but all were stronger than the year to follow. It was the last year for the SS and the big-block engines in Camaros, a distinction that makes a 1972 SS396 one desirable machine, especially since only 970 were sold.

The Z-28 was still the best performance car in the Camaro lineup, but enthusiasts started feeling ambivalent toward it. It was the Camaro with the most hair, but it was receding at the temples. It still had solid valve lifters and an aluminum intake manifold, but clearly the Z-28 was no longer race-ready in showroom trim.

Camaro production in 1972 was the lowest in its history, but viewed from a collector car standpoint, 68,651 is no small number. There are scarce models like the SS396 in there, but don't assume that 1972 Camaros are desirable simply because of that year's relatively low production.

The 1972 Camaro burned lower-octane fuel without complaint, it had great looks, and its quality of construction was generally good. Like the 1971 model, you should be picky about what you select. You'll pay less than you would for a 1970; about the same as a 1971 or 1973. The 1972 is not a sleeper—it won't explode in value. But if it serves your purposes, and the right car comes along, by all means give it consideration.

This was a correct 1972 Z-28 wheel, tire and center cap. Author photo.

CHAPTER 7
1973 Camaro

★★★ Z-28
★★★★ Z-28 with A/C
Add ◖ for Rally Sport

1973 Model Production: 96,751

After sales hit rock bottom in 1972, the Camaro started a mild recovery in 1973. This was the last Camaro model with the same exterior appearance as the car introduced in 1970. Through some engineering magic, the 1973 Camaro managed to squeak by the new bumper standards with little visual change. The standard front bumper came with rubber-faced, vertical guards, stronger mounting brackets, tubular reinforcing braces and a support bar tucked in behind the bumper itself. The same technology, sans the vertical guards, permitted the Rally Sport front end to continue, as well. Rear bumper brackets for all 1973 Camaros were strengthened and redesigned to provide an additional 0.4-inch space for bumper deflection.

The Camaro gained weight in 1973, as did most cars, but only sixteen pounds over 1972. With a curb weight of 3,229 pounds, the 1973 model was sixty-three pounds heavier than the 1970.

The Super Sport option was no longer available. The Camaro was evolving away from all-out performance to a more luxury-oriented market, so a new option called the Type LT (luxury touring) arrived. It included special identification and trim, concealed windshield wipers, left- and right-hand outside sport mirrors, seven-inch Rally wheels with caps and trim rings, sport steering wheel, deluxe seat trim, wood-grained door and instrument panel treatment, glove compartment lamp and special instrumentation (tach, ammeter, temperature gauge and electric clock).

Prior to 1973, the five-digit manufacturer's code, which also appeared in the VIN (vehicle identification number), was different for the six- and eight-cylinder models. In 1973, the base six- and eight-cylinder cars were the same (1FQ87), but Type LT models were 1FS87. The Type LT came with the RPO L65, 165-horsepower, 350-cubic-inch V-8. As with the Super Sport option of the previous year, you could upgrade the Type LT with the RPO L48 350-cubic-inch engine which had 175 horsepower in its 1973 version. But unlike the Super Sports, the Type LT could be combined with the Z-28. Or with the Rally Sport. Or with both.

Power windows became available as a midyear release in 1973. The power window controls were mounted in the console, itself a new design, so the console was a mandatory option with power windows.

You may recall that power windows were optional in 1967, 1968 and 1969 Camaros. But they weren't popular in the first generation. They reached their highest penetration, 2.2 percent, in the 1967 model year, so they weren't includ-

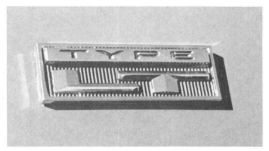

The Super Sport option was out, but the Type LT was in. It could be combined with the Rally Sport, the Z-28 or both. The standard front end needed vertical bumper guards to slip by the tougher 1973 front bumper standards. Author photos.

ed as optional in the 1970 model. Planners apparently concluded that the Camaro was being purchased as an economical sporty car, or a gung-ho street racer, neither of which required power window lifts. But each year of the seventies found the Camaro tilting more toward a convenience-minded market, so power windows came back in 1973 and continued to be optional in every Camaro to follow.

To give the 1973 Camaro more luggage room, a Space-Savr spare tire became optional. The stirrup-handle shift lever for automatic transmissions was replaced with a conventional, single-handle selector. The Powerglide two-speed automatic transmission was no longer available with any Camaro model.

The Z-28 was still around. It suffered in some respects, but gained in others. Solid valve lifters were gone, and the new hydraulic lifters wouldn't let the engine

1973 Camaro Colors/Options

Color Code	Body Color
11	Antique White
24	Light Blue
26	Dark Blue
29	Midnight Blue
42	Dark Green
44	Light Green
46	Green-Gold
48	Midnight Green
51	Light Yellow
56	Chamois
60	Light Copper
64	Silver
68	Dark Brown
74	Dark Red
75	Medium Red
97	Medium Orange

INTERIOR COLORS: Black, Chamois, Green, Neutral, Saddle

Order #	Item Description	Sticker $
1FQ87	Base Camaro Sport Coupe, 6-cyl	$2,780.70
1FQ87	Base Camaro Sport Coupe, V-8	2,871.70
1FS87	Base Camaro Type LT Coupe, V-8	3,267.70
AK1	Belts, Color-Keyed Seat and Shoulder	14.50
AN6	Seat Back, Adjustable	18.00
A01	Glass, Soft-Ray Tinted	39.00
A31	Power Windows	75.00
B37	Mats, Color-Keyed Floor	12.00
B84	Moldings, Body Side	33.00
B93	Moldings, Door Edge Guard	6.00
C08	Roof Cover, Vinyl	87.00
C24	Windshield Wipers, Hide-A-Way	21.00
C50	Defogger, Rear Window	31.00
C60	Air Conditioning, Four-Season	397.00
D34	Mirror, Visor Vanity	3.00
D35	Mirrors, Sport	26.00
D55	Console	57.00
D80	Spoilers, Front and Rear	77.00
D88	Stripes, Sport	77.00
F41	Suspension, Sport	30.00
G80	Axle, Positraction Rear	45.00
J50	Power Brakes	46.00
L48	Engine, 175-hp, 350-cid V-8 (w/Sp Cpe)	102.00
L48	Engine, 175-hp, 350-cid V-8 (w/LT)	76.00
L65	Engine, 145-hp, 350-cid V-8	26.00

Order #	Item Description	Sticker $
M20	Transmission, 4-Speed Wide Ratio	200.00
M21	Transmission, 4-Speed Close Ratio	200.00
M40	Transmission, Turbo Hydra-Matic	210.00
M40	Transmission, Turbo Hydra-Matic (w/Z28)	297.00
N33	Steering Wheel, Comfortilt	44.00
N40	Power Steering	113.00
N65	Spare Tire, Space Saver	14.16
N95	Wheel Trim, Wire Wheel Covers	82.00
PE1	Wheel Trim, Turbine I Wheels (w/Sp Cpe)	110.50
PE1	Wheel Trim, Turbine I Wheels (w/LT)	75.00
PO1	Wheel Trim, Bright Metal Wheel Covers	26.00
QEH	Tires, E78-14 Whitewall (w/N65)	22.40
QEH	Tires, E78-14 Whitewall (w/o N65)	28.00
QFC	Tires, F70-14 Whitewall (LT w/N65)	51.00
QFC	Tires, F70-14 Whitewall (LT w/o N65)	65.00
QFC	Tires, F70-14 Whitewall (Sp Cpe w/N65)	56.00
QFC	Tires, F70-14 Whitewall (Sp Cpe w/o N65)	70.00
QFD	Tires, E70-14 Lettered (LT w/N65)	61.40
QFD	Tires, F70-14 Lettered (LT w/o N65)	78.00
QFD	Tires, F70-14 Lettered (Sp Cpe w/N65)	66.40
QFD	Tires, F70-14 Lettered (Sp Cpe w/o N65)	83.00
T60	Battery, Heavy Duty	15.00
U14	Instrumentation, Special	82.00
U35	Clock, Electric	16.00
U63	Radio, AM	65.00
U69	Radio, AM-FM	135.00
U80	Speaker, Rear Seat	15.00
V01	Radiator, Heavy-Duty (w/o Z28)	14.00
V01	Radiator, Heavy-Duty (w/Z28)	7.50
YA7	Emission Equipment, California	15.00
YD1	Axle Ratio, Trailering	12.00
ZJ4	Trailer Towing Package	41.00
ZJ7	Wheel Trim, Rally Wheels	44.00
ZJ9	Lighting, Auxiliary	17.50
ZJ9	Lighting, Auxiliary (w/Z54 or LT)	15.00
Z21	Style Trim	56.00
Z22	Rally Sport Package (w/Sp Cpe)	118.00
Z22	Rally Sport Package (w/LT)	97.00
Z28	Special Performance Package (w/Sp Cpe)	598.05
Z28	Special Performance Package (w/LT)	502.05
Z54	Interior Decor/Quiet Sound Group	35.00

• Prices shown were introductory retail.

The Z-28 engine for 1973 used a Holley carburetor instead of a Rochester Quadrajet, switched from solid valve lifters to hydraulic, and could be combined with air conditioning for the first time. This made it the only second-generation Camaro that could combine the Z-28 and air conditioning with the original-style Rally Sport front end. By the way, the striped look of the air cleaner in this photo was from hood vent reflections. It was a smooth chrome finish. Author photos.

This scrumptious 1973 Z-28 had 99 miles on the odometer when photographed in late 1984, and the window sticker was still in place. How's that for a collector's dream? Author photo.

Do Camaros rust? Uh huh. The total annual cost of damage resulting from different kinds of corrosion in the United States is enormous. It cost $40 million to fix up the Statue of Liberty's rust problems. An article in the August 24, 1984, *Wall Street Journal* quoted a Battelle Memorial Institute study estimating that annual corrosion costs in the United States are equal to 4.9 percent of its gross national product. That's big, and Camaros have been in there contributing their fair share. So be careful. A refurbished Camaro might look great on the surface, but look further. It may be structurally shot. Author photos.

1973 Camaro

BASE ENGINE (SIX CYLINDER)

Type: . . . . Chevrolet ohv inline 6
Bore x stroke, inches: 3.875x3.53
Displacement, inches: 250
Compression ratio: 8.25:1
Horsepower: .100 @ 3600 rpm
Torque: . . . . .175 @ 1600 rpm
Distributor: . . . . Single point breaker
Other engines offered: . .The base V-8 was 307-cid with 115-hp. Additional V-8 engines of 350-cid were available with power ratings from 145-hp to 245-hp.

CHASSIS AND DRIVETRAIN

Clutch: . . . . Single dry-plate

Transmission: . . .Three speed manual standard. Four-speed manual and three-speed automatic optional.
Front suspension: . .Coil springs, tube-type shock absorbers
Rear suspension: . .Leaf springs, tube-type shock absorbers
Axle ratio: 3.08:1
Frame: . . . . .Box section front subframe, unibody rear

GENERAL

Wheelbase, inches: 108.0
Height, inches: 49.1
Width, inches: 74.4
Length, inches: 188.5
Brakes, standard: . . . . .Disc front, drum rear
Wheels: . . . . .Steel
Body material: . . . . .Steel
Tire size, base: E78-14
Fuel capacity, gallons: 18.0

rev as high. Power dropped from 255 horsepower at 5600 rpm to 245 horsepower at 5200 rpm in 1973. But the change to hydraulic lifters permitted air conditioning to be ordered with the Z-28 for the first time in the Camaro's history. Chevrolet hadn't offered air with the Z-28 earlier because solid-lifter engines could rev higher and spin air-conditioning belts off or turn the air compressor too fast.

Other Z-28 changes included a Holley four-barrel carburetor to replace the Rochester Quadrajet, a cast-iron intake manifold to replace aluminum, and a lower price. In fact, thanks mainly to the rollback of the federal excise tax in late 1971, a similarly equipped 1973 Camaro cost less than a 1971.

The Camaro had become an eye-opening bargain, and *Car and Driver* realized it. In a test appearing in the September 1973 issue, *Car and Driver* featured a Camaro Type LT Z-28 and said, "With a price tag that's actually decreased, it's a

This 1973 Camaro was factory-equipped with the RPO U80 rear speaker and the RPO C50 rear window defogger. The defogger was the forced-air type, and Camaros used them until the in-glass style came along in 1979. The defogger was activated by a two-position toggle switch under the lighter. Author photos.

The 1973 Z-28 still had cast emblems on the side fenders, but the rear panel emblem had been changed to thin adhesive foil beginning with the 1972 model. Author photos.

In 1973, customers selected from a base six-cylinder, a base 307-cubic-inch V-8, or three 350-cubic-inch V-8's (one was standard in the Type LT, another in the Z-28). Even though the Z-28 was a 350, it got a Z-28 emblem in place of this numerical one. Author photo.

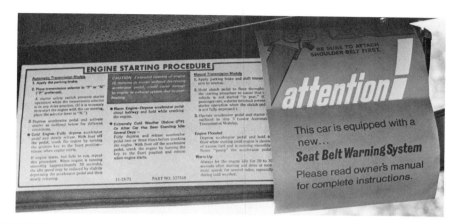

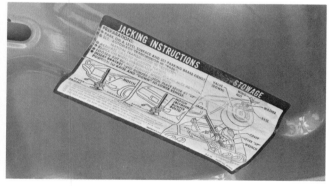

Enthusiasts like decals, stickers and ID tags to be in place, and the 1973 had plenty. Examples included the permanent engine-starting label stuck inside the sun visor, slip-on seatbelt warning card, tire pressure and manufacturer's labels on the door jamb, trim tag on the upper firewall ledge visible by lifting the hood, and the jacking instructions label on the inner trunk surface. Author photos.

The Custom Interior option that Camaro enthusiasts had come to know disappeared in 1973, but most of what it contained were rolled into the Type LT, including this door panel. The design was different in detail only, like brighter wood-graining, from its 1972 counterpart. Author photo.

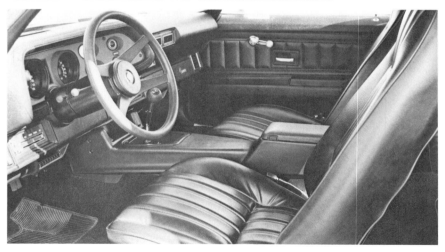

This 1973 base interior did have some extra-cost items like the new-design RPO D55 console, RPO D35 sport mirrors with remote control on the driver's side and tilt steering wheel (RPO N33). The four-spoke steering wheel was optional in 1971 and 1972, but standard in 1973. This car didn't have them, but power windows (RPO A31) were added to the option list late in 1973, and Chevrolet sold 217 sets. Author photos.

blue chip investment in a world of inflation." The editors felt that compared to a 1971, the Z-28 had suffered in throttle response but was equal in every other way. With a 0-60 time of 6.7 seconds, it's important to realize that the 1973 Z-28 was still a heck of a performer.

Nineteen seventy-three was a transition year for Camaros. The 1970 was the last of the high-compression, pure-performance Camaros. With the 1971 and 1972 models, Chevrolet held on as best it could, building similar Camaros aimed at the same mission, but with compromises in power, thanks to Uncle Sam.

By 1973, Chevrolet realized the Camaro had no choice but to tilt away from brute performance toward convenience and luxury. So it decided to roll with the tide and make the best of it. The result was a Camaro model that offered some interesting possibilities.

The Rally Sport styling introduced in 1970 was in a world of its own; the 1973 Camaro was the last year for the Rally Sport with that beautiful front end.

The 1973 Camaro was the first that could combine air conditioning with the Z-28 package. And the new Type LT could be ordered with both Rally Sport and Z-28. This was exactly the car that so impressed *Car and Driver* in its September 1973 test. It also had four-speed manual transmission, rear defogger, vanity mirror (another "luxury" option, but hardly extravagant at $3), deluxe seatbelts, AM-FM radio, rear speaker, adjustable seatback, front and rear spoiler and tilt steering wheel. The car listed for $4,855.25 — one terrific value!

For investment, the car just described tops the 1973 list. Any Z-28 with air is desirable, but a *real* Rally Sport Z-28 with air was possible only in 1973.

Of all Camaro models, a properly equipped 1973 comes closest to being a sleeper. Generally, car enthusiasts think of 1973 cars as real bow-wows. It was a year of some ugly stop-gap measures to meet bumper requirements, added weights, engines that ran better after the key was shut off, and horrible fuel economy because gas was cheap and King Faisal was still a few months away from initiating the first oil crisis.

Through a quirk of fate, the Camaro slid under most of this. It weighed a few extra pounds but still looked fabulous. Option combinations were possible that hadn't been before and wouldn't be again. Its engine stumbled some, but once it caught on, look out!

If your neighbor has a pristine 1973 Z-28 Rally Sport with air that might be for sale, best wander over there right now. Then again, you probably wouldn't like it. Call me.

CHAPTER 8
1974-1977 Camaro

★★★ 1977 Z-28
★★★★ 1974 Z-28

1974 Model Production: 151,008
1975 Model Production: 145,770
1976 Model Production: 182,959
1977 Model Production: 218,853

The four Camaro models grouped in this chapter looked similar, but significant things happened during the 1974-77 period. The Rally Sport and Z-28 options both departed, then returned. Mandatory use of no-lead fuel and catalytic converters made their debut. The Camaro finally outsold the Mustang in annual sales.

The styling of the 1974-77 Camaros was marked by the addition of aluminum bumpers front and rear, a body-colored fascia above the front bumper, and new taillights. Chevrolet managers chose the aluminum bumper system to meet the tougher 1974 bumper standards. Weight *was* added, but the aluminum saved fifty pounds per car compared to steel bumpers. These Camaros were seven inches longer than earlier second-generation models.

By 1974, bumper standards were dictating what designers could and couldn't do. It was expensive enough designing one new system that would qualify, let alone two. So the Rally Sport option, which had always had its own distinct front end styling, was dropped for the 1974 Camaro model year.

Engine selection for 1974 was limited but confusing. The base RPO L22 six, with 250 cubic inches and 100 horsepower, continued. The base V-8 engine of the previous year, the 307-cubic-inch, was discontinued. In its place was the 350-cubic-inch, 145-horsepower RPO L65 V-8. However, this engine hadn't been certified for California, so the base V-8 there was the RPO LM1, a 350-cubic-inch engine with 160 horsepower. Californians had to pay an extra $46 for their V-8, which could be purchased *only* in California. The RPO L48 350-cubic-inch V-8 with 185 horsepower was optional in all states for 1974 Camaros, and was ten horsepower higher than its 1973 version.

The Z-28 was available in all states for 1974. Its 350 V-8 developed 245 horsepower (the same as in 1973), and the package included finned aluminum rocker covers, bright accents, heavy-duty cooling, RPO J50 power brakes, dual exhausts, black-finish grille, emblems on front fenders, sport suspension, heavy-duty starter and clutch, 15x7-inch wheels with bright lug nuts, special center caps and trim rings, F60x15-inch bias-belted ply white-letter tires and Positraction axle. If air conditioning was ordered with the Z-28, the rear axle ratio was 3.42:1; without air, the axle ratio was 3.73:1. A breakerless ignition General Motors called High Energy Ignition (HEI) became part of the Z-28 during the 1974 production run. Optional wild hood and rear deck striping was unique to the Z-28. It was RPO D88, with color choices of red, white, blue, and black. The cost was $77.

All 1974 V-8 Camaros came with power steering at no extra cost. A new fuel

Any doubt this 1974 Camaro is a Z-28? Author photo.

The Z-28 was in every Camaro model lineup from 1967 through 1974, but then it was dropped. It was revived in 1977, but some enthusiasts still think the 1974 was the last of the true Z's. There was no doubt it was a handsome machine. It and all 1974 models received new aluminum bumpers front and rear, and sheet-molded-compound (SMC) plastic facias, painted body color, at both ends. This Z-28 had the optional RPO D80 front and rear spoiler set, available on any Camaro that year. As before, the flexible front spoiler was shipped inside the car for installation by the dealer. Sales of the spoiler sets hit 19,104 in 1974. Author photos.

tank adapted from the Nova increased capacity from eighteen to twenty-one gallons. (Speaking of fuel, this was the last Camaro to legally burn leaded regular.)

Radial tires became available for the first time with the 1974 Camaros. Sensors were added to the front brakes to warn of pad wear. Keying was changed, so that the square ignition key no longer fit the doors.

Nineteen seventy-four Camaros had the infamous seatbelt interlock system. This required front seat passengers to buckle up before the car would start. In Camaros, sensors under the front seat told the system when someone was sitting in the seat (a heavy bag of groceries would fool the sensor); another sensor in the seatbelt buckle informed the system when it was okay to start the car. Even

1974 Camaro Colors/Options

Color Code	Body Color
11	Antique White
26	Bright Blue
29	Midnight Blue
36	Aqua Blue
40	Lime Yellow
46	Bright Green
49	Medium Dark Green
50	Cream Beige
51	Bright Yellow
53	Light Gold
55	Sandstone
59	Golden Brown
64	Silver
66	Bronze
74	Medium Red (Metallic)
75	Medium Red

INTERIORS: Black, Green, Neutral, Red, Saddle, Taupe

Order #	Item Description	Sticker $
1FQ87	Base Camaro Sport Coupe, 6-cyl	2,827.70
1FQ87	Base Camaro Sport Coupe, V-8	3,039.70
1FS87	Base Camaro Type LT Coupe, V-8	3,380.70
AK1	Belts, Color-Keyed Seat and Shoulder	14.50
AN6	Seat Back, Adjustable	18.00
A01	Glass, Soft-Ray Tinted	39.00
A31	Power Windows	75.00
B37	Mats, Color-Keyed Floor	12.00
B84	Moldings, Body Side	33.00
B93	Moldings, Door Edge Guard	6.00
C08	Roof Cover, Vinyl	87.00
C24	Windshield Wipers, Hide-A-Way	21.00
C50	Defogger, Rear Window	31.00
C60	Air Conditioning, Four-Season	397.00
D34	Mirror, Visor Vanity	3.00
D35	Mirrors, Sport	26.00
D55	Console	57.00
D80	Spoilers, Front and Rear	77.00
D88	Striping	77.00
F41	Suspension, Sport	30.00
G80	Axle, Positraction Rear	45.00
J50	Power Brakes	46.00
LM1	Engine, 160-hp, 350-cid V-8	46.00
L48	Engine, 185-hp, 350-cid V-8	76.00
M20	Transmission, 4-Speed Wide Ratio	200.00
M21	Transmission, 4-Speed Close Ratio	200.00

Order #	Item Description	Sticker $
M40	Transmission, Turbo Hydra-Matic	210.00
M40	Transmission, Turbo Hydra-Matic (w/Z28)	297.00
N33	Steering Wheel, Comfortilt	44.00
N41	Power Steering	113.00
N65	Spare Tire, Space Saver	14.16
PE1	Wheel Trim, Turbine I Wheels (w/Sp Cpe)	110.50
PE1	Wheel Trim, Turbine I Wheels (w/LT)	75.00
P01	Wheel Trim, Bright Metal Wheel Covers	26.00
QBT	Tires, FR78-14 Lettered (w/o N65)	147.15
QBT	Tires, FR78-14 Lettered (Sp Cpe w/N65)	117.72
QBT	Tires, FR78-14 Lettered (LT w/N65)	116.72
QDV	Tires, FR78-14 Blackwall (w/o N65)	104.15
QDV	Tires, FR78-14 Blackwall (Sp Cpe w/N65)	83.32
QDV	Tires, FR78-14 Blackwall (LT w/N65)	82.32
QDW	Tires, FR78-14 Whitewall (w/o N65)	134.15
QDW	Tires, FR78-14 Whitewall (Sp Cpe w/N65)	107.32
QDW	Tires, FR78-14 Whitewall (LT w/N65)	106.32
QEH	Tires, E78-14 Whitewall (Sp Cpe w/N65)	22.40
QEH	Tires, E78-14 Whitewall (Sp Cpe w/o N65)	28.00
QFC	Tires, F70-14 Whitewall (Sp Cpe w/N65)	56.00
QFC	Tires, F70-14 Whitewall (Sp Cpe w/o N65)	70.00
QFD	Tires, F70-14 Lettered (Sp Cpe w/N65)	66.40
QFD	Tires, F70-14 Lettered (Sp Cpe w/o N65)	83.00
UA1	Battery, Heavy-Duty	15.00
U05	Horns, Dual	4.00
U14	Instrumentation, Special	82.00
U35	Clock, Electric	16.00
U58	Radio, AM-FM Stereo	233.00
U63	Radio, AM	65.00
U69	Radio, AM-FM	135.00
U80	Speaker, Rear Seat	15.00
V01	Radiator, Heavy-Duty (w/o Z28)	14.00
V01	Radiator, Heavy-Duty (w/Z28)	7.50
V30	Guards, Front and Rear Bumper	31.00
YF5	Emission Equipment, California	15.00
ZJ4	Trailer Towing Package	41.00
ZJ7	Wheel Trim, Rally Wheels	44.00
ZJ9	Lighting, Auxiliary	17.50
ZJ9	Lighting, Auxiliary (w/Z54 or LT)	15.00
Z21	Style Trim	52.00
Z28	Special Performance Package (w/Sp Cpe)	572.05
Z28	Special Performance Package (w/LT)	502.05
Z54	Interior Decor/Quiet Sound Group	35.00

• Prices shown were introductory retail.

faithful seatbelt users hated the interlock, and the government rescinded the regulation the following year.

The Type LT had proven to be popular, so it was upgraded further in 1974. Seats were redone in new fabrics, interior detailing was revised, and Amberlite sound insulation was added inside the doors and rear quarters, under carpets, behind the rear seat and under the rear package shelf.

Styling for 1975 changed little, except for a new rear window that wrapped around the sides of the roof. The smaller window would get the stylist's vote, but the new window increased rear vision, a shortcoming in the earlier cars.

To the eye, the 1975 Camaro looked similar, but that year had the nebulous honor of being the first with a catalytic converter, thus the first to require unleaded fuel. To prevent the use of leaded fuel, the filler neck was made smaller to accept only the narrow unleaded pump nozzle, and Unleaded Fuel Only warning labels appeared.

Engine selection dwindled even further. From the fourteen available in 1969, the Camaro was down to three in 1975—make that two, if you lived in California. The base six remained the 250-cubic-inch engine, with a horsepower increase from 100 to 105. The base V-8 was again the RPO L65 350 with 145 horsepower. As in 1974, this wasn't certified for California, but the RPO LM1 350 V-8 with 155 horsepower was. The RPO LM1 could be purchased in all states.

That was it for engines, because the Z-28 was gone. Later on, Chevrolet executives would say it was a matter of conscience; if they couldn't build the Z-28 the way they wanted, they wouldn't build it at all. More likely, it was simply a marketing decision, based on the incorrect assumption that the performance car market was gone. The Firebird Trans Am continued through this period with great success. Chevrolet realized its error, and the Z-28 was back for 1977½.

The high-energy breakerless ignition, phased-in midyear with the 1974 Z-28, became standard equipment on all 1975 Camaros. For the first time, air conditioning could be combined with a six-cylinder Camaro engine. Radial tires designed by GM became standard equipment also, but bias-belted tires could be

The Type LT in sedate trim was a nice looker, too. The 1974 Camaros were the last to feature the rear window shape introduced in 1970, and also the last to burn leaded fuel. Chevrolet photo.

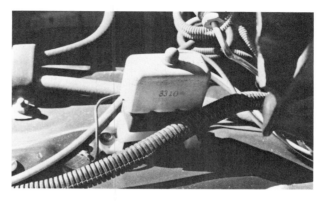

Nineteen-seventy-four was the year for the infamous seat-belt interlock system that required engaging the seatbelts before the car would start. If the system's logic got scrambled and refused to permit starting even when everyone was properly buckled-in, someone had to lift the hood and push the reset button shown above. The 1974 was the only model year with this reset device, and even though everyone hated the interlock, collectors insist the system be intact. Author photo.

This was the Z-28 engine for 1974, essentially unchanged from 1973. It still had finned aluminum valve covers, bright accents, dual-snorkel air cleaner and 245 horsepower. General Motor's new high-energy breakerless ignition was added to Z-28's during 1974 production. There were 13,802 Z-28 Camaros sold in 1974. Author photo.

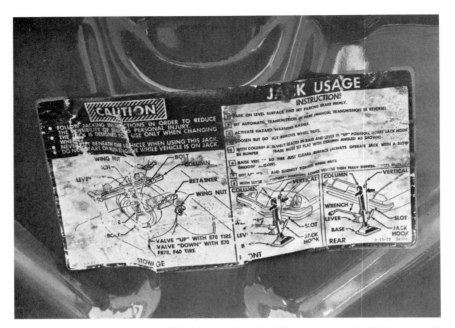

The 1974's new bumpers required a new jacking instructions label. The wire entering the deck lid at the left was for the trunk light, part of the RPO ZJ9 auxiliary lighting package. Author photos.

ordered as delete options. Power door locks became optional for the first time on 1975 Camaros.

The big news for 1975 was the return of the Rally Sport option. It wasn't what it used to be—no hidden headlights like the first generation, no snout grilles like the early second generation. The Rally Sport of 1975 was a paint-and-stripe package, but a nice one if you liked that sort of thing. Introduced in midyear, it included blacked-out treatment for hood, header panel, grille, headlamp bezels, top surface of front fender, forward portion of roof, upper portion of door and side windows, rear end panel and license opening; tricolor striping separating black from body color at roof and side and front fenders; tricolor Rally Sport decals on front fender and deck lid. This package was RPO Z85 at $238 with the Sport Coupe, or $165 with the Type LT.

For a short while in 1975, genuine leather trim for the Type LT appeared as optional for $216. It was the only time leather seating had ever been optional for any first- or second-generation Camaro.

An RPO F40 suspension option for $17 included special front and rear shocks and springs, but 1975 Camaros could also have a Gymkhana suspension with seven-inch wheels, E60x15-inch white-letter tires, front and rear stabilizers, heavy-duty front and rear shocks, plus a special steering ratio.

There isn't too much to say about bicentennial 1976. The Camaro looked the same, other than a bright aluminum rear fascia and "leather look" for the instru-

The 1975 Camaro got a new appearance thanks to the larger rear window. Noticeable exterior appearance options on this Type LT included RPO PE1 turbine wheels ($75), and RPO V30 front and rear bumper guards. The breakerless ignition phased-in with 1974 Z-28's became standard on all 1975 Camaros. All 1975 models received the catalytic converter, and with it the requirement to use unleaded fuel. Chevrolet photos.

ment panel around the gauges, both with the Type LT. California residents could get the same engines as in other states, but the choices were just three: The base six-cylinder continued unchanged, the base V-8 was a new 305-cubic-inch engine with 140 horsepower, and the 350 V-8 (RPO LM1) continued, but with ten additional horsepower at 165.

Power brakes became standard on all Camaro V-8 models in 1976, and cruise control (called Speed Control, RPO K30) could be ordered for the first time on a second-generation Camaro. A new-style vinyl roof left a painted band at the rear, capturing a little of the reincarnated Rally Sport look.

In 1976, Camaro sales reached 182,959, the highest so far of the second generation.

1975 Camaro Colors/Options

Color Code	Body Color
11	Antique White
13	Silver
15	Light Gray
24	Medium Blue
26	Bright Blue
29	Midnight Blue
44	Medium Green
49	Dark Green
50	Cream Beige
51	Bright Yellow
55	Sandstone
58	Dark Sandstone
63	Light Saddle
64	Medium Orange
74	Dark Red
75	Light Red

INTERIOR COLORS: Medium Graystone, Dark Red, Dark Saddle, Medium Sandstone

Order #	Item Description	Sticker $
1FQ87	Base Camaro Sport Coupe, 6-cyl	3,553.05
1FQ87	Base Camaro Sport Coupe, V-8	3,698.05
1FS87	Base Camaro Type LT Coupe, V-8	4,070.05
AK1	Belts, Color-Keyed Seat and Shoulder	16.00
AN6	Seat Back, Adjustable	18.00
AU3	Door Lock System, Power	56.00
A01	Glass, Soft-Ray Tinted	45.00
A31	Power Windows	91.00
B37	Mats, Color-Keyed Floor	14.00
B84	Moldings, Body Side	38.00
B93	Moldings, Door Edge Guard	7.00
C09	Roof Cover, Vinyl	87.00
C24	Windshield Wipers, Hide-A-Way	21.00
C50	Defogger, Rear Window	41.00
C60	Air Conditioning, Four-Season	435.00
D34	Mirror, Visor Vanity	3.00
D35	Mirrors, Sport	27.00
D55	Console	68.00
D80	Spoilers, Front and Rear	77.00
D88	Striping (Black)	77.00
FE8	Suspension, Radial Tuned	35.00
G80	Axle, Positraction Rear	49.00
G92	Axle, High Altitude	12.00
G95	Axle, Highway	12.00

Order #	Item Description	Sticker $
J50	Power Brakes	55.00
LM1	Engine, 155-hp, 350-cid V-8	54.00
M20	Transmission, 4-Speed Wide Ratio	219.00
M40	Transmission, Turbo Hydra-Matic	235.00
N33	Steering Wheel, Comfortilt	49.00
N65	Spare Tire, Space Saver	14.10
PE1	Wheel Trim, Turbine I Wheels (w/Sp Cpe)	110.50
PE1	Wheel Trim, Turbine I Wheels (w/LT)	75.00
P01	Wheel Trim, Bright Metal Wheel Covers	30.00
QBT	Tires, FR78-14 Lettered	46.00
QDW	Tires, FR78-14 Whitewall	33.00
QEG	Tires, E78-14 Blackwall (Sp Cpe w/N65)	−105.42
QEG	Tires, E78-14 Blackwall (Sp Cpe w/o N65)	−105.90
QEH	Tires, E78-14 Whitewall (Sp Cpe w/N65)	−74.42
QEH	Tires, E78-14 Whitewall (Sp Cpe w/o N65)	−74.90
UA1	Battery, Heavy-Duty	15.00
UM1	Radio, AM, Stereo Tape	199.00
UM2	Radio, AM-FM Stereo, Tape	363.00
U05	Horns, Dual	4.00
U14	Instrumentation, Special	88.00
U35	Clock, Electric	17.00
U58	Radio, AM-FM Stereo	233.00
U63	Radio, AM	69.00
U69	Radio, AM-FM	135.00
U80	Speaker, Rear Seat	19.00
V01	Radiator, Heavy-Duty (w/o Z28)	15.00
V30	Guards, Front and Rear Bumper	34.00
YF5	Emission Equipment, California	45.00
ZJ7	Wheel Trim, Rally Wheels	46.00
ZJ9	Lighting, Auxiliary	22.50
ZJ9	Lighting, Auxiliary (w/Z54 or LT)	20.00
Z08	Sports Decor Package (Sp Cpe w/Z21)	40.00
Z08	Sports Decor Package (Sp Cpe w/o Z21)	42.00
Z08	Sports Decor Package (LT w/Z21)	13.00
Z08	Sports Decor Package (LT w/o Z21)	15.00
Z21	Style Trim	55.00
Z54	Interior Decor/Quiet Sound Group	35.00
Z85	Rally Sport (w/Sp Cpe)	238.00
Z85	Rally Sport (w/LT)	165.00
Z86	Suspension, Gymkhana (w/o Z85)	112.00
Z86	Suspension, Gymkhana (w/Z85)	66.00
Z86	Suspension, Gymkhana (w/LT)	66.00

• Prices shown were introductory retail.

The Rally Sport was discontinued in 1974 because of the new bumper design, but returned in 1975. But there were no hidden headlights as in the first Camaro generation, no snout grilles and European-style turn lamps as in the early second generation. No, the resurrected Rally Sport was a paint and trim option. The 1976 shown here displayed the blacked-out front and rear treatment, and note the unleaded fuel warning that started with the 1975. Incidentally, the cockeyed taillight was normal. Author photos.

1976 Camaro Colors/Options

Color Code	Body Color
11	Antique White
13	Silver
19	Black
28	Light Blue
35	Dark Blue
36	Firethorn
37	Mahogany
40	Lime Green
49	Dark Green
50	Cream
51	Bright Yellow
65	Buckskin
67	Medium Saddle
78	Medium Orange

INTERIOR COLORS: Black, Dark Firethorn, Light Buckskin, White/Black, White/Blue, White/Lime, White/Dark Firethorn

Order #	Item Description	Sticker $
1FQ87	Base Camaro Sport Coupe, 6-cyl	3,762.35
1FQ87	Base Camaro Sport Coupe, V-8	3,927.35
1FS87	Base Camaro Type LT Coupe, V-8	4,320.35
AK1	Belts, Color-Keyed Seat and Shoulder	17.00
AN6	Seat Back, Adjustable	19.00
AU3	Door Lock System, Power	62.00
A01	Glass, Soft-Ray Tinted	46.00
A31	Power Windows	99.00
B37	Mats, Color-Keyed Floor	15.00
B80	Moldings, Roof Drip	16.00
B84	Moldings, Body Side	38.00
B93	Moldings, Door Edge Guard	7.00
C24	Windshield Wipers, Hide-A-Way	22.00
C50	Defogger, Rear Window	43.00
C60	Air Conditioning, Four Season (w/6-cyl)	470.00
C60	Air Conditioning, Four Season (w/V-8)	452.00
D35	Mirrors, Sport	27.00
D55	Console	71.00
D80	Spoilers, Front and Rear	81.00
F41	Suspension, Sport	32.00
G80	Axle, Positraction Rear	51.00
G92	Axle, High Altitude	13.00
J50	Power Brakes	58.00
K30	Cruise Control	73.00

Order #	Item Description	Sticker $
LM1	Engine, 165-hp, 350-cid V-8	85.00
M20	Transmission, 4-Speed Wide Ratio	242.00
M21	Transmission, 4-Speed Close Ratio (w/Z28)	n/c
M40	Transmission, Turbo Hydra-Matic	260.00
N33	Steering Wheel, Comfortilt	57.00
N65	Spare Tire, Stowaway (w/o radials)	15.11
N65	Spare Tire, Stowaway (w/radials)	−1.13
PE1	Custom Style Wheels (w/o Z85)	116.00
PE1	Custom Style Wheels (w/Z85)	79.00
PE1	Custom Style Wheels (w/LT)	79.00
P01	Full Wheel Covers	30.00
QBT	Tires, FR78-14 Lettered (w/N65)	39.00
QBT	Tires, FR78-14 Lettered (w/o N65)	49.00
QDW	Tires, FR78-14 Whitewall (w/N65)	28.00
QDW	Tires, FR78-14 Whitewall (w/o N65)	35.00
QEG	Tires, E78-14 Blackwall (w/N65)	−84.40
QEG	Tires, E78-14 Blackwall (w/o N65)	−105.75
QEH	Tires, E78-14 Whitewall (w/N65)	−72.75
QEH	Tires, E78-14 Whitewall (w/o N65)	−58.40
UA1	Battery, Heavy-Duty	16.00
UM1	Radio, AM, Stereo Tape	209.00
UM2	Radio, AM-FM Stereo, Tape	324.00
U05	Horns, Dual	6.00
U14	Instrumentation, Special	92.00
U35	Clock, Electric	18.00
U58	Radio, AM-FM Stereo	226.00
U63	Radio, AM	75.00
U69	Radio, AM-FM	137.00
U76	Windshield Antenna (incl w/radios)	16.00
U80	Speaker, Rear Seat	21.00
V01	Radiator, Heavy Duty	27.00
V30	Guards, Front and Rear Bumper	36.00
YF5	Emission Equipment, California	50.00
ZJ7	Wheel Trim, Rally Wheels	60.00
ZJ9	Lighting, Auxiliary	30.00
ZJ9	Lighting, Auxiliary (w/Z54 or LT)	26.00
Z21	Style Trim	58.00
Z54	Interior Decor/Quiet Sound Group	53.00
Z85	Rally Sport (w/Sp Cpe)	260.00
Z85	Rally Sport (w/LT)	173.00

• Prices shown were introductory retail.

The 1976 Camaro received interior refinements, but the exterior, save a nice brushed trim panel for the Type LT's rear, was a duplicate of 1975. Even so, Camaro sales reached 182,959, the highest yet for any second-generation model. Chevrolet photos.

Things started getting interesting again in 1977. Styling was little changed, but the Z-28 returned in midyear. It wasn't an engine option package, but rather a separate model, the Z-28 Sport Coupe, joining the Sport Coupe and Type LT Coupe.

The emphasis of the new Z-28 was on suspension and graphics. The suspension had front and rear stabilizer bars, special spring rates and shock valving, and faster steering. The graphics included body-colored wheels, spoilers, mirrors and bumpers; blacked-out grille, rear-end panel, head- and tail lamp bezels, rocker panels, moldings and license opening; hood decal; wheelhouse and rocker panel accent stripes, decals and emblems. The retail price of the Z-28 Sport Coupe was $5,170.60.

Engines remained similar to the previous year, though different horsepower ratings were given for those sold in California. The base six-cylinder crept up another five horsepower to 110 from 105 horsepower, except in California, where it was just 90 horsepower. The RPO LG3 305-cubic-inch V-8 rated 135 horsepower in California, 145 horsepower elsewhere. The RPO LM1, the 350-cubic-inch V-8, was 160 horsepower in California, 150 horsepower in the other states. The Z-28 engine stood at 185 horsepower and 350 cubic inches. Four-speed transmissions were not sold in California in 1977.

Through the 1974-77 period, magazines generally grumbled about the sad state of affairs afflicting the auto industry, but complimented Chevrolet for continuing to build Corvettes and Camaros with enthusiasts in mind. So when the Z-28 came back in 1977½, they really gave it a warm welcome. Chevrolet management had touted the Z-28 suspension as being the equal of any, and writers admitted it was extremely good. In an April 1977 comparison article featuring the Z-28 and Firebird Trans Am, *Car and Driver* said, "Rather than let the proud name become just another plastic applique on the flanks of various ordinary cars—as happened to the Pontiac GTO and Plymouth Road Runner—Chevrolet yanked the car off the market. Now it returns in a fashion that is sure to blow the lid off the entire world of fast automobiles and end, once and for all, the notion that Detroit and the American public have forgotten performance."

The Z-28 and Firebird Trans Am comparison was judged a dead heat, with the only noteworthy item of superiority being the Firebird's steering wheel.

Other items of interest for 1977 Camaros were the addition of intermittent windshield wipers as an option, Type LT availability with the six-cylinder engine, hidden windshield wipers as standard equipment for all Camaros, and a new shift pattern for the four-speed manual transmission, which repositioned the reverse location. Last, 1977 was the year the Camaro finally outsold its archrival, the Mustang, by 198,755 to 161,654.

The 1974-77 Camaros shouldn't be thought of in investment-collector car terms. Some will depreciate less than other cars, some may even appreciate a little. But these were compromised cars; cars that sold very well because Chevrolet did a better job of compromising than the competition, what little there was. It took the American auto manufacturers until the early eighties to come to grips with federal mandates and to build clean-sheet-approach cars that both the government and auto enthusiasts could learn to love.

Still, there are interesting cars in the 1974-77 Camaro grouping, and several that at the least would make excellent drivers, especially for the pittance some now cost. Here are the pros and cons.

The 1977 Camaro looked like the 1976 which looked like the 1975. But Chevrolet was doing something right because the 1977 again set a second-generation sales record at 218,959. And a new Z-28, this one with the emphasis on handling, came back in mid-year. Chevrolet photos.

1977 Camaro Colors/Options

Color Code	Body Color
11	Antique White
13	Silver
19	Black
22	Light Blue
29	Dark Blue
36	Firethorn
38	Aqua
44	Medium Green
51	Bright Yellow
61	Light Buckskin
63	Buckskin (Metallic)
69	Brown
75	Light Red
78	Orange

INTERIOR COLORS: Black, Blue, Buckskin/Black, Buckskin/Saddle, Firethorn, Firethorn/Black, White/Aqua, White/Black, White/Blue, White/Firethorn, White/Saddle

Order #	Item Description	Sticker $
1FQ87	Base Camaro Sport Coupe, 6-cyl	4,113.45
1FS87	Base Camaro Type LT, 6-cyl	4,478.45
1FQ87	Z28 Camaro Sport Coupe, V-8	5,170.06
AK1	Belts, Color-Keyed Seat and Shoulder	19.00
AN6	Seat Back, Adjustable	20.00
AU3	Door Lock System, Power	68.00
A01	Glass, Soft-Ray Tinted	50.00
A31	Power Windows	108.00
B37	Mats, Color-Keyed Floor	16.00
B80	Moldings, Roof Drip	17.00
B84	Moldings, Body Side	40.00
B93	Moldings, Door Edge Guard	8.00
CD4	Windshield Wipers, Intermittent	30.00
C50	Defogger, Rear Window	48.00
C60	Air Conditioning, Four Season (w/6-cyl)	507.00
C60	Air Conditioning, Four Season (w/V-8)	478.00
D35	Mirrors, Sport	30.00
D55	Console	75.00
D80	Spoilers, Front and Rear	87.00
F41	Suspension, Sport	36.00
G80	Axle, Positraction Rear	54.00
G92	Axle, Performance Ratio	14.00
J50	Power Brakes	61.00
K30	Cruise Control	80.00
LG3	Engine, 145-hp, 305-cid V-8 (135-hp Cal)	120.00

Order #	Item Description	Sticker $
LM1	Engine, 170-hp, 350-cid V-8 (160-hp Cal)	210.00
M20	Transmission, 4-Speed Wide Ratio	252.00
M21	Transmission, 4-Speed Close Ratio (w/Z28)	n/c
M40	Transmission, Turbo Hydra-Matic	282.00
M40	Transmission, Turbo Hydra-Matic (w/Z28)	30.00
NA6	Emissions, High Altitude	22.00
N33	Steering Wheel, Comfortilt	57.00
N65	Spare Tire, Stowaway	n/c
PE1	Custom Style Wheels (w/o Z85)	125.00
PE1	Custom Style Wheels (w/Z85)	85.00
PE1	Custom Style Wheels (w/LT)	85.00
P01	Full Wheel Covers	33.00
QBT	Tires, FR78-14 Lettered (w/N65)	44.00
QBT	Tires, FR78-14 Lettered (w/o N65)	55.00
QDW	Tires, FR78-14 Whitewall (w/N65)	33.00
QDW	Tires, FR78-14 Whitewall (w/o N65)	41.00
QEG	Tires, E78-14 Blackwall (w/N65)	−86.94
QEG	Tires, E78-14 Blackwall (w/o N65)	−107.10
QEH	Tires, E78-14 Whitewall (w/N65)	−55.94
QEH	Tires, E78-14 Whitewall (w/o N65)	−68.10
UA1	Battery, Heavy-Duty	17.00
UM1	Radio, AM, Stereo Tape	209.00
UM2	Radio, AM-FM Stereo, Tape	324.00
U05	Horns, Dual	6.00
U14	Instrumentation, Special	99.00
U35	Clock, Electric	19.00
U58	Radio, AM-FM Stereo	226.00
U63	Radio, AM	72.00
U69	Radio, AM-FM	137.00
U76	Windshield Antenna (incl w/radios)	17.00
U80	Speaker, Rear Seat	23.00
V01	Radiator, Heavy-Duty	29.00
V30	Guards, Front and Rear Bumper	39.00
YF5	Emissions Equipment, California	70.00
ZJ7	Wheel Trim, Rally Sport	65.00
ZJ9	Lighting, Auxiliary	32.00
ZJ9	Lighting, Auxiliary (w/Z54 or LT)	27.00
Z21	Style Trim	61.00
Z54	Interior Decor/Quiet Sound Group	57.00
Z85	Rally Sport (w/Sp Cpe)	281.00
Z85	Rally Sport (w/LT)	186.00

• Prices shown were introductory retail.

If you like the styling of one, you like them all, because the only change of significance is the larger rear window of the 1975 and later models. I don't think the window makes a dollar's difference in value. A 1974 wouldn't be worth less because of its small window, nor would the later cars command proportionally more. The second-generation Camaro was designed with the smaller window and looks best that way, yet the larger glass area does seem to fit with the car's evolution. It's a tossup.

These were the heaviest Camaros ever. The 1974 weighed 3,429 pounds, the 1975 3,531 pounds, the 1976 3,513 pounds, and the 1977 3,456 pounds. (As with power ratings in this text, these are manufacturer's figures and have to be taken with a grain of salt.) They were all too heavy, the 1975 being the champ, but you wouldn't rule out one of these on weight alone. If you're after the fuel efficiency that comes with light weight, nothing in this span of Camaros will entice you.

The 1974 Camaro was the last to legally burn leaded regular fuel, and it will run today without much complaint—save some dieseling—on the cheapest pump grades. And the Z-28 (what was left of it) was still alive in 1974.

The 1975 didn't have the Z-28, but it did get the Rally Sport back in midyear.

The 1976 Camaro has hardly any claim to fame, yet it was the best single sales year for the Camaro second generation . . . until the 1977.

Nineteen seventy-seven saw the return of the Z-28, with a new emphasis on handling. Some of these have depreciated to practically nothing, and many represent tremendous driving values for the money. The suspension was first-rate, it had bumpers that looked like bumpers, and it seems to run forever. Buy one of these right, give it reasonable care, and you can probably enjoy several years of depreciation-free driving.

1974-77 Camaro

BASE ENGINE (SIX CYLINDER)

Type: . . . . .Chevrolet ohv inline 6
Bore x stroke, inches: .3.875x3.53
Displacement, inches: 250
Compression ratio: . . . . .8.25:1 (8.3:1 in 1977)
Horsepower: .100 (1974), 105 (1975-76), 110 (1977 except Calif which was 90)
Torque: . . . . . 175 (1974), 185 (1975-76), 195 (1977 except Calif which was 180)
Distributor: . . . . . .Single point breaker (1974), high energy breakerless ignition (1975-77)
Other engines offered: . .The base V-8 was 350-cid with 145-hp in 1974-75, except California where the base V-8's were not available. The base V-8 was 305-cid with 140-hp in 1976. All V-8's were optional in 1977. The additional V-8 engines available from 1974 through 1977 had displacements of 305-cid and 350-cid and power ratings from 135-hp to 245-hp.

CHASSIS AND DRIVETRAIN

Clutch: . . . . .Single dry-plate
Transmission: . . .Three speed manual standard. Four-speed manual and three-speed automatic optional.
Front suspension: . .Coil springs, tube-type shock absorbers
Rear suspension: . .Leaf springs, tube-type shock absorbers
Axle ratio: 3.08:1 (1974), 2.73:1 (1975-77)
Frame: . . . . .Box section front subframe, unibody rear

GENERAL

Wheelbase, inches: 108.0
Height, inches: 49.1
Width, inches: 74.4
Length, inches: 195.4
Brakes, standard: . . . . .Disc front, drum rear
Wheels: . . . . .Steel
Body material: . . . . .Steel
Tire size, base: E78-14 (1974), FR78-14 (1975-77)
Fuel capacity, gallons: 21.0

CHAPTER 9
1978-1981 Camaro

 Z-28

1978 Model Production: 272,631
1979 Model Production: 282,571
1980 Model Production: 152,005
1981 Model Production: 126,139

The 1978, 1979, 1980 and 1981 Camaros shared a new appearance created by the third and final facelift of the second generation. All had soft, body-colored fronts and rears, with new grille and taillight designs. Considering this was quite different from what stylists originally had in mind when the second generation was created, the new look worked out well.

These are the Camaros you see every day on the highway, and on practically every used-car lot. Sales ranged from a new record high to a near record low thanks to the second Middle East oil crisis. The third facelift was intended to bridge the gap between the 1978 and the all-new Camaro due in 1982. These Camaros did that, generally selling well against the competition, maintaining the enthusiast following developed over several years, and bringing new customers in with an ever-expanding option selection of comfort and convenience features. By 1981, a customer could equip a Camaro with six different radios, power assists on everything but seats, a wide variety of wheels, wheelcovers and tires, and removable glass roof panels.

For 1978, the Camaro came in five basic models: Sport Coupe, Rally Sport Coupe, Type LT Coupe, LT Rally Sport Coupe and Z-28 Sport Coupe.

The 1978 engines were much the same as 1977. The base six continued with the RPO L22 250 of 90 horsepower for California and 110 horsepower in other states. The RPO LG3, a 305 V-8, had 135 horsepower in California and 145 horsepower elsewhere. The RPO LM1, the 350-cubic-inch V-8, had 160 horsepower in California, ten more in other states. The Z-28 version of the 350-cubic-inch V-8 had 170 horsepower in California and 175 horsepower in other states. No manual transmissions could be purchased in California Camaros.

Other improvements for 1978 included a better-isolated exhaust system for the six, added front frame reinforcements and redesigned rear spring shackles for better stability, a noncorroding nylon brake-pressure differential switch to replace the old steel one, and a charcoal filter to absorb corrosive fumes in the power brake booster vacuum line. You got the impression that Chevrolet was fine tuning a well-proven chassis.

Important new options for 1978 included removable glass roof panels (RPO CC1 at $625) and aluminum road wheels.

Axle ratios were lowered across the board for better fuel economy, the 305-cubic-inch-displacement engine came with a four-speed manual transmission included in its price instead of a three-speed manual, and the Z-28 got a simulated string-wrapped steering wheel.

Camaro Berlinetta, circa 1981. Chevrolet photo.

The 1978 featured a new look created by a major restyling of the front and rear, the second-generation's second facelift. The Rally Sport pictured here in action continued to feature anything-but-subtle paint graphics. Removable roof panels (RPO CC1) hit the Camaro option sheets for the first time in 1978 and Chevrolet sold 9,875 sets. As the trend to luxury continued, interiors got ever more plush. Chevrolet photos.

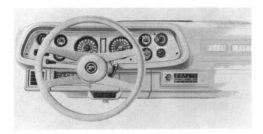

The instrument panel for 1978 had the look of the previous year except for detail changes like the string-wrapped steering wheel for Z-28 models. The Z-28 itself was back to stay, and in 1978 it featured a lot of specific trim such as side fender vents and a unique hood. Chevrolet photos.

Car and Driver's Don Sherman liked the 1978 Z-28, commenting, "The knife edge of acceleration and handling is blunted, but ride, styling and interior comfort are all honed to a new brilliance."

Customers must have agreed with Sherman, because the 1978 Camaro shellacked the Mustang in sales, 247,437 to 179,039. It was a new record year for any Camaro. Even Europeans recognized the Camaro as an exceptional performance value; it was the best-selling American car in West Germany in 1978.

In 1979, the Type LT was replaced by the Berlinetta. The four base Camaros became the Sport Coupe, Rally Sport Coupe, Berlinetta Sport Coupe and Z-28 Sport Coupe.

1978 Camaro Colors/Options

Color Code	Body Color
11	White
15	Silver
19	Black
22	Light Blue
24	Bright Blue
34	Orange-Yellow
48	Dark Blue-Green
51	Bright Yellow
63	Camel
67	Saffron
69	Dark Camel
75	Light Red
77	Carmine

INTERIOR COLORS: Black, Blue, Camel, Carmine, Green, White/Black, White/Blue, White/Carmine, White/Green, White/Saffron

Order #	Item Description	Sticker $
1FQ87	Camaro Sport Coupe	4,414.25
1FQ87	Z85 Camaro Rally Sport Coupe	4,784.25
1FS87	Camaro Type LT Coupe	4,814.25
1FS87	Z85 Camaro Type LT Rally Sport Coupe	5,065.25
1FQ87	Z28 Camaro Sport Coupe	5,603.85
AK1	Belts, Color-Keyed Seat and Shoulder	21.00
AN6	Seat Back, Adjustable	21.00
AU3	Door Lock System, Power	80.00
A01	Glass, Soft-Ray Tinted	56.00
A31	Power Windows	124.00
B37	Mats, Color-Keyed Floor	20.00
B80	Moldings, Roof Drip	23.00
B84	Moldings, Body Side	42.00
B93	Moldings, Door Edge Guard	11.00
CC1	Roof Panels, Removable Glass	625.00
CD4	Windshield Wipers, Intermittent	32.00
C50	Defogger, Rear Window	51.00
C60	Air Conditioning, Four Season (w/o V-8)	539.00
C60	Air Conditioning, Four Season (w/V-8)	508.00
D35	Mirrors, Sport	33.00
D55	Console	80.00
D80	Spoiler, Rear	55.00
F41	Suspension, Sport	38.00
G80	Axle, Positraction Rear	59.00
G92	Axle, Performance Ratio	15.00
J50	Power Brakes	69.00
K30	Cruise Control	90.00
LG3	Engine, 145-hp, 305-cid V-8 (135-hp Cal)	185.00
LM1	Engine, 170-hp, 350-cid V-8 (160-hp Cal)	300.00
MM4	Transmission, 4-Speed Wide Ratio	125.00

Order #	Item Description	Sticker $
MX1	Transmission, Automatic (w/Sp Cpe & LT)	307.00
MX1	Transmission, Automatic (w/Z28)	45.00
M21	Transmission, 4-Speed Close Ratio (w/Z28)	n/c
NA6	Emissions, High Altitude	33.00
N33	Steering Wheel, Comfortilt	69.00
N65	Spare Tire, Stowaway	n/c
PE1	Custom Style Wheels (w/Sp Cpe)	133.00
PE1	Custom Style Wheels (w/LT or RS)	91.00
PO1	Full Wheel Covers	37.00
QBT	Tires, FR78-14 Lettered(w/N65)	49.00
QBT	Tires, FR78-14 Lettered (w/o N65)	61.00
QDW	Tires, FR78-14 Whitewall (w/N65)	37.00
QDW	Tires, FR78-14 Whitewall (w/o N65)	46.00
QEG	Tires, E78-14 Blackwall (w/N65)	−89.56
QEG	Tires, E78-14 Blackwall (w/o N65)	−112.95
QEH	Tires, E78-14 Whitewall (w/N65)	−54.56
QEH	Tires, E78-14 Whitewall (w/o N65)	−68.95
UA1	Battery, Heavy-Duty	18.00
UM1	Radio, AM, Stereo Tape	229.00
UM2	Radio, AM-FM Stereo, Tape	328.00
U05	Horns, Dual	7.00
U14	Instrumentation, Special	106.00
U35	Clock, Electric	20.00
U58	Radio, AM-FM Stereo	229.00
U63	Radio, AM	79.00
U69	Radio, AM-FM	149.00
U76	Windshield Antenna (incl w/radios)	25.00
U80	Speaker, Rear Seat	24.00
V01	Radiator, Heavy-Duty	31.00
YF5	Emission Equipment, California	75.00
YJ8	Wheels, Color-Keyed Aluminum (w/Sp Cpe)	265.00
YJ8	Wheels, Color-Keyed Aluminum (w/Z28)	195.00
YJ8	Wheels, Color-Keyed Aluminum (w/RS-LT)	180.00
ZJ7	Wheel Trim, Rally Wheels	85.00
ZJ9	Lighting, Auxiliary	34.00
ZJ9	Lighting, Auxiliary (w/Z54 or LT)	28.00
Z21	Style Trim	70.00
Z54	Interior Decor/Quiet Sound Group	61.00
J--2	Cloth Seats (w/Sp Cpe, Z28)	21.00
F--2	Custom Cloth Seats (w/LT)	21.00
F--2	Custom Cloth Seats (w/Z28)	315.00
S--2	Custom Sport Cloth Seats (w/LT)	21.00
S--2	Custom Sport Cloth Seats (w/Z28)	315.00
X--2	Custom Vinyl Seats (w/Z28)	294.00

• Prices shown were introductory retail.

The 1979 engines were exactly as those of 1978, other than minor power rating changes (both up and down as emissions grew tighter, but engineers found ways to stave off the effects). Again, manual transmissions and California were mutually exclusive.

The marketing people juiced up the 1979 Camaro with new paint colors and interior fabrics—the usual fare—but the car looked the same as before . . . until you saw the instrument panel: same gauges and layout, but set in a new, more

1979 Camaro Colors/Options

Color Code	Body Color
11	White
15	Silver
19	Black
22	Light Blue
24	Bright Blue
29	Dark Blue
40	Light Green
44	Medium Green
51	Bright Yellow
61	Beige
63	Camel
69	Dark Brown
75	Red
77	Carmine

INTERIOR COLORS: Black, Blue, Camel, Carmine, Green, Oyster/Gray

Order #	Item Description	Sticker $
1FQ87	Camaro Sport Coupe	4,676.90
1FQ87	Z85 Camaro Rally Sport Coupe	5,072.90
1FS87	Camaro Berlinetta Coupe	5,395.90
1FQ87	Z28 Camaro Sport Coupe	6,115.35
AK1	Belts, Color-Keyed Seat and Shoulder	23.00
AN6	Seat Back, Adjustable	23.00
AU3	Door Lock System, Power	86.00
A01	Glass, Soft-Ray Tinted	64.00
A31	Power Windows	132.00
B37	Mats, Color-Keyed Floor	23.00
B80	Moldings, Roof Drip	24.00
B84	Moldings, Body Side	43.00
B93	Moldings, Door Edge Guard	13.00
CC1	Roof Panels, Removable Glass	655.00
CD4	Windshield Wipers, Intermittent	38.00
C49	Defogger, Rear Window	99.00
C60	Air Conditioning, Four Season (w/o V-8)	562.00
C60	Air Conditioning, Four Season (w/V-8)	529.00
D35	Mirrors, Sport	43.00
D55	Console	80.00
D80	Spoiler, Rear	58.00
F41	Suspension, Sport	41.00
G80	Axle, Positraction Rear	64.00
G92	Axle, Performance Ratio	18.00
J50	Power Brakes	76.00
K30	Cruise Control	103.00
LG3	Engine, 135-hp, 305-cid V-8 (130-hp Cal)	235.00
LM1	Engine, 170-hp, 350-cid V-8 (165-hp Cal)	360.00
MM4	Transmission, 4-Speed Wide Ratio	135.00
MX1	Transmission, Automatic	335.00
MX1	Transmission, Automatic (w/Z28)	59.00
M21	Transmission, 4-Speed Close Ratio (w/Z28)	n/c

Order #	Item Description	Sticker $
N33	Steering Wheel, Comfortilt	75.00
N65	Spare Tire, Stowaway	n/c
N90	Wheels, Aluminum (w/Berl)	172.00
N90	Wheels, Aluminum (w/Sp Cpe)	315.00
N90	Wheels, Aluminum (w/Z28)	242.00
N90	Wheels, Aluminum (w/RS)	222.00
PE1	Custom Style Wheels (w/Sp Cpe)	143.00
PE1	Custom Style Wheels (w/RS)	100.00
P01	Full Wheel Covers	43.00
QBT	Tires, FR78-14 Ltr (w/o Berl, w/N65)	52.00
QBT	Tires, FR78-14 Ltr (w/o Berl, w/o N65)	65.00
QBT	Tires, FR78-14 Ltr (w/Berl, w/N65)	13.00
QBT	Tires, FR78-14 Ltr (w/Berl, w/o N65)	16.00
QDW	Tires, FR78-14 Whitewall (w/N65)	40.00
QDW	Tires, FR78-14 Whitewall (w/o N65)	49.00
QEG	Tires, E78-14 Blackwall (w/N65)	−94.56
QEG	Tires, E78-14 Blackwall (w/o N65)	−118.95
QEH	Tires, E78-14 Whitewall (w/N65)	57.56
QEH	Tires, E78-14 Whitewall (w/o N65)	71.95
TR9	Lighting, Auxiliary	37.00
TR9	Lighting, Auxiliary (w/Berl or Z54)	31.00
UA1	Battery, Heavy-Duty	20.00
UM1	Radio, AM, Stereo Tape	248.00
UM2	Radio, AM-FM Stereo, Tape	335.00
UN3	Radio, AM-FM Stereo, Cassette	341.00
UP5	Radio, AM-FM, CB	489.00
UP6	Radio, AM-FM Stereo, CB	570.00
UY8	Radio, AM-FM Stereo, Clk	395.00
UY8	Radio, AM-FM St, clk (w/Z28, U14, Berl)	372.00
U05	Horns, Dual	9.00
U14	Instrumentation, Special	112.00
U35	Clock, Electric	23.00
U58	Radio, AM-FM Stereo	232.00
U63	Radio, AM	85.00
U69	Radio, AM-FM	158.00
U75	Power Antenna	47.00
U76	Windshield Antenna	27.00
U80	Speaker, Rear Seat	25.00
V01	Radiator, Heavy-Duty	33.00
YF5	Emission Equipment, California	83.00
ZJ7	Wheel Trim, Rally Wheels	93.00
Z21	Style Trim	73.00
Z54	Interior Decor/Quiet Sound Group	64.00
J--2	Cloth Seats (w/Sp Cpe, RS, Z28)	23.00
S--2	Custom Cloth Seats (w/Berl)	23.00
S--2	Custom Cloth Seats (w/Sp Cpe, RS, Z28)	330.00
X--2	Custom Vinyl Seats (w/Sp Cpe, RS, Z28)	307.00

• Prices shown were introductory retail.

Amid all this talk of high performance and luxury, one must remember that the base transmission for Camaros remained a three-speed manual throughout the second generation. Cracked dashes were a problem in second-generation Camaros and they didn't have to be very old, as this photo of a 1978 shows. Author photos.

Chevrolet eliminated the Type LT in 1979 and brought in the Berlinetta. This left four base models; Sport Coupe, Rally Sport Coupe, Berlinetta and Z-28 Sport Coupe. Each was a separate model and they couldn't be combined. Chevrolet photo.

The 1979 Camaro marked the tenth year of the second generation, so Chevrolet treated it to a beautiful new instrument cluster. Controls and instruments were in similar locations, but the appearance was more contemporary. Note the Z-28 emblem filling the window crank hole in this power-window-equipped model. Author photos.

contemporary, flat-mounting design. A new in-glass electric rear-window defogger became optional for the first time in Camaros (a forced-air blower-type disappeared after 1978) and the radio options grew to include cassette tape decks combined with AM-FM stereos, citizen band units combined with AM-FM stereos and AM-FM stereos with digital clocks. Electric fender-mount and in-windshield antennas were available. The 1979 Z-28 got a wild new front air dam that wrapped into the forward part of the front wheelwells.

Engines were juggled considerably for the 1980 Camaro, mostly in the quest for better fuel economy. The in-line-six engine was gone, replaced by two 3.8-liter V-6's. In California, the base V-6 was the RPO LD5, built by Buick and having 231 cubic inches of displacement and 110 horsepower. In other states, the base V-6 was a Chevrolet-built engine (RPO LC3) with 229-cubic-inch displacement and 115 horsepower. There was a new, small V-8 with 120 horsepower and 267-cubic-inch displacement, but not for Californians. The RPO LG4, a 305-cubic-inch V-8, was available in all states. The RPO LM1 with 350-cubic-inch displacement was the Z-28 engine, but wasn't certified for California sale. If a Z-28 was ordered for California, it came with the RPO LG4 (305) and a $50 credit. Again, no manual transmissions for California.

Sales in 1980 plunged to 152,005, this on the heels of Chevrolet projections of a new record in the area of 280,000. The Camaro had been on a roll, but the

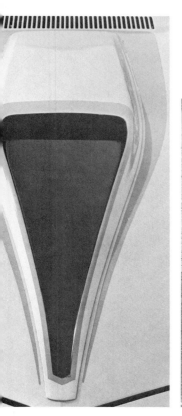

The 1979 Z-28 had a unique bolt-on hood scoop and blacked-out front end treatment. Rally Sport and Z-28 models included the RPO D80 rear spoiler in their prices, but it was available with any Camaro. Sales of Z-28's in 1979 reached 84,877; the Rally Sport sold 19,101 units. For what it's worth, 81 customers selected a little-known option called RPO VE1 which deleted the rear spoilers from their Z-28 or Rally Sport. Author photos.

world was in its second Middle East oil crisis and the U.S. was depressed about the Iranian hostage mess, record inflation and interest rates. In short, the country wasn't in a buying mood, and the American auto industry plunged into its worst and longest recession. Considering its age, the Camaro actually held on well in a very confused world.

The Z-28 for 1980 got a new, functional, rear-facing hood scoop. It fed cold air through a flap triggered electrically at full throttle. The Z-28 also received functional side fender ports for exiting hot engine air plus rear fender flares to go with the front ones added in 1979.

Chevrolet has always had a way with words and here's what it had to say about the 1980 Rally Sport: "CHEVROLET CAMARO RALLY SPORT FOR 1980 . . . features new thin-line grille styling, and new standard, power-efficient lightweight V6 engine. Two optional engines—4.4-liter and 5.0-liter V8s—are also new to the model. A new Rally Sport grille is shared by the standard Camaro and Berlinetta models. Manual and automatic transmissions are offered with the 3.3-liter V6 and 5.0-liter engines, but only an automatic is available with the smaller V8. The V6 engine is about 60 pounds lighter, smaller and more compact than the in-line six it replaces, yet it produces equivalent horsepower. The standard engine with automatic transmission utilizes a new torque converter clutch system that eliminates slippage in 'drive' range and saves energy. (The system is not available in California.)" Chevrolet photo.

We shouldn't ignore the Berlinetta. It continued as the luxo-Camaro, and new, wire wheelcovers became standard. It and all other 1980 Camaros had slightly reworked grille designs.

The 1981 Camaro was the last of the second generation. Engineers did a lot of tweaking to squeeze better fuel economy from what had simply become a car too heavy for the payload delivered.

Engines remained much the same for 1981, but Californians could finally get a 350-cubic-inch V-8. They could also get four-speed sticks, but nobody could get

1980 Camaro Colors/Options

Color Code	Body Color
11	White
15	Silver
19	Black
24	Bright Blue
29	Dark Blue
40	Lime Green
51	Bright Yellow
57	Gold
67	Dark Brown
72	Red
76	Dark Claret
79	Red Orange
80	Bronze
84	Charcoal

INTERIOR COLORS: Black, Blue, Camel, Carmine, Oyster

Order #	Item Description	Sticker $
1FP87	Camaro Sport Coupe	5,498.60
1FP87	Z85 Camaro Rally Sport Coupe	5,915.60
1FS87	Camaro Berlinetta Coupe	6,261.60
1FP87	Z28 Camaro Sport Coupe	7,121.32
AN6	Seat Back, Adjustable	25.00
AU3	Door Lock System, Power	93.00
A01	Glass, Soft-Ray Tinted	68.00
A31	Power Windows	143.00
B37	Mats, Color-Keyed Floor	25.00
B80	Moldings, Roof Drip	26.00
B84	Moldings, Body Side	46.00
B93	Moldings, Door Edge Guard	14.00
CC1	Roof Panels, Removable Glass	695.00
CD4	Windshield Wipers, Intermittent	41.00
C49	Defogger, Rear Window	107.00
C60	Air Conditioning, Four Season	566.00
D35	Mirrors, Sport	46.00
D80	Spoiler, Rear	62.00
F41	Suspension, Sport	44.00
G80	Axle, Positraction Rear	68.00
G92	Axle, Performance Ratio	19.00
J50	Power Brakes	81.00
K30	Cruise Control	112.00
LG4	Engine, 155-hp, 305-cid V-8	295.00
LG4	Engine, 165-hp, 305 cid V-8 (w/Z28)	−50.00
LM1	Engine, 190-hp, 350-cid V-8 (w/Z28)	n/c
L39	Engine, 120-hp, 267-cid V-8	180.00
MM4	Transmission, 4-Speed Wide Ratio	144.00
MM4	Transmission, 4-Speed Wide Ratio (w/Z28)	n/c
MX1	Transmission, Automatic	358.00
MX1	Transmission, Automatic (w/Z28)	63.00

Order #	Item Description	Sticker $
N33	Steering Wheel, Comfortilt	81.00
N65	Spare Tire, Stowaway	n/c
N90	Wheels, Aluminum (w/Berl)	184.00
N90	Wheels, Aluminum (w/Sp Cpe)	337.00
N90	Wheels, Aluminum (w/RS)	237.00
N90	Wheels, Aluminum (w/Z28)	257.00
PE1	Custom Style Wheels (w/Sp Cpe)	153.00
PE1	Custom Style Wheels (w/RS)	107.00
P01	Full Wheel Covers	46.00
QGR	Tires, P255/70R-15 Lettered (w/Z28)	n/c
QJY	Tires, P205/75R-14 WW (w/Berl)	n/c
QJY	Tires, P205/75R-14 WW (w/o Berl, w/N65)	51.00
QJY	Tires, P205/75R-14 WW (w/o Berl, w/o N65)	63.00
QKL	Tires, P205/75R-14 Ltr (w/o Berl, w/N65)	65.00
QKL	Tires, P205/75R-14 Ltr (w/o Berl, w/o N65)	81.00
QKL	Tires, P205/75R-14 Ltr (w/Berl, w/N65)	15.00
QKL	Tires, P205/75R-14 Ltr (w/Berl, w/o N65)	18.00
TR9	Lighting, Auxiliary	40.00
TR9	Lighting, Auxiliary (w/Berl or Z54)	33.00
UA1	Battery, Heavy-Duty	21.00
UM1	Radio, AM, Stereo Tape (8-track)	249.00
UM2	Radio, AM-FM Stereo, Tape (8-track)	272.00
UN3	Radio, AM-FM Stereo, Cassette	285.00
UP5	Radio, AM-FM, CB	473.00
UP6	Radio, AM-FM Stereo, CB	525.00
UY8	Radio, AM-FM Stereo, Clk	353.00
UY8	Radio, AM-FM St, Clk (w/Z28, U14, Berl)	328.00
U05	Horns, Dual	10.00
U14	Gage Package with Tachometer	120.00
U35	Clock, Electric	25.00
U58	Radio, AM-FM Stereo	192.00
U63	Radio, AM	97.00
U69	Radio, AM-FM	153.00
U75	Power Antenna	51.00
U76	Windshield Antenna	27.00
U80	Speaker, Rear Seat	20.00
V08	Cooling, Heavy-Duty (w/o C60)	63.00
V08	Cooling, Heavy-Duty (w/C60)	36.00
YF5	Emissions Equipment, California	250.00
ZJ7	Wheel Trim, Rally Wheels	100.00
Z21	Style Trim	78.00
Z54	Interior Decor/Quiet Sound Group	69.00
C--2	Cloth Seats (w/Sp Cpe, RS, Z28)	25.00
F--2	Custom Cloth Seats (w/Berl)	25.00
F--2	Custom Cloth Seats (w/Sp Cpe, RS, Z28)	353.00
X--2	Custom Vinyl Seats (w/Sp Cpe, RS, Z28)	328.00

• Prices shown were introductory retail.

These photos of a 1981 model show several features and options that crept into the second generation. A single-handle, automatic shifter replaced the stirrup style in 1973 for Camaros with consoles. Power door locks (button above door handle) made the option list in 1975. Optional power windows arrived in mid-1973 and required the console because that's where the controls were mounted, and the rear window defogger switch activated the new in-glass-element defogger that made its debut in 1979. Author photos.

The advent of self-serve gasoline stations prompted Chevrolet to move the filler neck from behind the license plate, where it had been in previous Camaros through the 1977 model, to a more convenient location behind the little door located between the taillights. The door also concealed the trunk release. Chevrolet photo.

The on-again, off-again Rally Sport was off again for 1981, and the Camaro was down to three basic models: Sport Coupe, Berlinetta (shown) and Z-28. Chevrolet finally created three distinct Camaro models with three easily definable missions: The base Coupe was the no-frills unit for the budget minded. The Berlinetta was the luxo cruiser. And the Z-28 was the performance machine. Simple. Chevrolet photos.

the combination of the 350 V-8 plus a four-speed. The RPO LM1 350-cubic-inch came only with automatic. Officially, this was the Z-28 engine, but the automatic had to be added for $61. For a four-speed Z-28, the engine had to be the 305-cubic-inch-displacement RPO LG4. As in 1980, Californians couldn't get the little RPO L39 V-8 with 267-cubic-inch displacement.

The Rally Sport was also deleted in 1981, so there were then three base cars: Sport Coupe, Berlinetta Sport Coupe and Z-28 Sport Coupe. A lock-up torque converter came with all the automatic transmissions, working in second and third gears in the Z-28, and third gear only for all others. Power brakes, previously standard only with the Z-28, became standard equipment with all Camaros. The Space-Savr spare tire, an option since 1973, also became standard on all models. Locks for the wire wheelcovers of the Berlinetta (RPO N18) were optional at $34.

1981 Camaro Colors/Options

Color Code	Body Color
11	White
16	Silver
19	Black
20	Bright Blue
21	Light Blue
29	Dark Blue
51	Bright Yellow
54	Gold
57	Orange
67	Dark Brown
75	Red
77	Maroon
84	Charcoal

INTERIOR COLORS: Beige, Black, Dark Blue, Red, Silver

Order #	Item Description	Sticker $
1FP87	Camaro Sport Coupe	6,581.23
1FS87	Camaro Berlinetta Coupe	7,356.23
1FP87	Z28 Camaro Sport Coupe	8,025.23
AN6	Seat Back, Adjustable	24.00
AU3	Door Lock System, Power	93.00
A01	Glass, Soft-Ray Tinted	75.00
A31	Power Windows	140.00
B37	Mats, Color-Keyed Floor	25.00
B80	Moldings, Roof Drip	25.00
B84	Moldings, Body Side	44.00
B93	Moldings, Door Edge Guard	13.00
CC1	Roof Panels, Removable Glass	695.00
CD4	Windshield Wipers, Intermittent	41.00
C49	Defogger, Rear Window	107.00
C60	Air Conditioning, Four Season	560.00
D35	Mirrors, Sport	47.00
D80	Spoiler, Rear	60.00
F41	Suspension, Sport	43.00
G80	Axle, Positraction Rear	67.00
G92	Axle, Performance Ratio	19.00
K35	Cruise Control w/Resume	132.00
LG4	Engine, 150-hp, 305-cid V-8	50.00
LG4	Engine, 165-hp, 305-cid V-8 (w/Z28)	n/c
LM1	Engine, 175-hp, 350-cid V-8 (w/Z28)	std
L39	Engine, 115-hp, 267-cid V-8	50.00
MM4	Transmission, 4-Speed Wide Ratio	141.00
MM4	Transmission, 4-Speed Wide Ratio (w/Z28)	n/c

Order #	Item Description	Sticker $
MX1	Transmission, Automatic	349.00
MX1	Transmission, Automatic (w/Z28)	61.00
N18	Wheel Cover Locks	34.00
N33	Steering Wheel, Comfortilt	81.00
N90	Wheels, Aluminum (w/Berl)	180.00
N90	Wheels, Aluminum (w/Sp Cpe)	331.00
N90	Wheels, Aluminum (w/Z28)	253.00
PE1	Custom Style Wheels	151.00
PO1	Full Wheel Covers	46.00
QGR	Tires, P225/70R-15 Ltr (w/Z28)	n/c
QJY	Tires, P205/75R-14 WW (w/Berl)	n/c
QJY	Tires, P205/75R-14 WW (w/o Berl)	54.00
QKL	Tires, P205/75R-14 (w/Berl)	15.00
QKL	Tires, P205/75R-14 (w/o Berl)	69.00
TR9	Lighting, Auxiliary	39.00
TR9	Lighting, Auxiliary (w/Berl or Z54)	33.00
TT4	Halogen Headlights	36.00
UA1	Battery, Heavy-Duty	20.00
UM2	Radio, AM-FM Stereo w/8-track	252.00
UN3	Radio, AM/FM Stereo w/cassette	264.00
UP6	Radio, AM-FM Stereo w/CB	487.00
U05	Horns, Dual	10.00
U14	Gage Package with Tachometer	118.00
U35	Clock, Electric	23.00
U58	Radio, AM-FM Stereo	178.00
U63	Radio, AM	90.00
U69	Radio, AM-FM	142.00
U75	Power Antenna	47.00
U76	Windshield Antenna	25.00
U80	Speaker, Rear Seat	19.00
V08	Cooling, Heavy-Duty (w/o C60)	61.00
V08	Cooling, Heavy-Duty (w/C60)	34.00
YF5	Emissions Equipment, California	46.00
ZJ7	Wheel Trim, Rally Wheels	99.00
Z21	Style Trim	76.00
Z54	Interior Decor/Quiet Sound Group	67.00
C--2	Cloth Seats (w/Sp Cpe, Z28)	26.00
F--2	Custom Cloth Seats (w/Berl)	26.00
F--2	Custom Cloth Seats (w/Sp Cpe, Z28)	330.00
X--2	Custom Vinyl Seats (w/Sp Cpe, Z28)	304.00

• Prices shown were introductory retail.

Here's the last of the second-generation Z-28 models, the 1981, complete with functional side-fender air scoops, functional solenoid-operated air induction hood scoop, and special graphics. The RPO N90 aluminum wheels were extra at $331 with the Z-28, more with other models. Author photos top; Chevrolet photo bottom.

The standard wheel for the 1981 Z-28 was the 15x7 Sport Wheel shown here. It was painted the body color. The 1981 Camaro ended the second generation with sales of 126,139, of which 43,272 wore the Z-28 nameplates. Chevrolet photo.

1978-81 Camaro

BASE ENGINE (SIX CYLINDER)

Type: . . Chevrolet ohv inline 6 (1978-79), ohv V-6 (1980-81)

Bore x stroke, inches: . . . 3.875x3.53 (1978-79), 3.74x3.48 (1980-81 except Calif at 3.80x3.40)

Displacement, inches: . 250 (1978-79), 229 (1980-81 except Calif at 231)

Compression ratio: . . 8.1:1 (1978), 8.0:1 (1979 except Calif at 8.2:1), 8.6:1 (1980-81 except Calif at 8.0:1)

Horsepower: . . . 110 (1978 except Calif at 90), 115 (1979-80 except Calif at 90 in 1979, 110 in 1980), 110 (1981)

Torque: . . . 195 (1978 except Calif at 175), 200 (1979 except Calif at 175), 175 (1980 except Calif at 190), 170 (1981 except Calif at 190)

Distributor: . . . . High energy ignition (breakerless)

Other engines offered: . . . . V-8 engines were available in displacements of 267-cid, 305-cid, and 350-cid with power ratings from 115-hp to 190-hp.

CHASSIS AND DRIVETRAIN

Clutch: . . . . Single dry-plate

Transmission: . Three speed manual. Four-speed manual and three-speed automatic optional.

Front suspension: . . Coil springs, tube-type shock absorbers

Rear suspension: . . Leaf springs, tube-type shock absorbers

Axle ratio: . . . 2.73:1 (1978), 2.56:1 (1979-81 except Calif at 2.73:1).

Frame: . . . . Box section front subframe, unibody rear

GENERAL

Wheelbase, inches: 108.0

Height, inches: 49.2

Width, inches: 74.4 (1978), 74.5 (1979-81)

Length, inches: 195.5 (1978), 197.6 (1979-81)

Brakes, standard: . . . . . . Disc front, drum rear (power assist standard in 1981)

Wheels: . . . . Steel

Body material: . . . . Steel

Tire size, base: . . . . FR78-14 (1978-79, E78-14 available as delete cost option), P195/75R-14 (1980), P205/75R-14 (1981)

Fuel capacity, gallons: 21.0 (1978), 20.8 (1979-81)

Halogen headlamps could be substituted for the standard sealed beams with RPO TT4 at $36.

The 1978-81 Camaros are strictly used cars today—not collector cars, not investment cars. However, they *are* enthusiast cars, or at least some are. All-out performance for these years (really, for all Camaros after 1971) plots like a Dow-Jones chart for a declining stock market. There are blips upward here and there as engineers learned new ways to pull power from increasingly emission-strangled engines, but the overall trend was one of decline. Camaros suffered through the period with a beautiful body designed in the late sixties; beautiful, but too heavy for a changed world.

The Berlinettas of this period became superb personal luxury cars with above-average handling. The Z-28's were superb-handling cars with plenty of luxury. I rank the cars of this period as better looking than the aluminum-bumper models of 1974-77, but not in the same league as the 1970-73 Camaros.

I can't recommend one of these years over the other. Generally, someone ordering a new car with the intention of selling it within a few years is best advised to avoid any option that doesn't specifically add value according to one of the guides dealers use, like the NADA (National Automobile Dealers' Association) monthly guide. Conversely, when you're looking at used cars, the loaded models don't sell for as high a percentage of their original sticker, and they're the best bargains. That's my view, but I happen to like options. The other view is that more options, especially motor-driven ones, mean there are more things to go wrong, especially in a used car. To each his own.

What the 1978-81 Camaros do offer is very refined everyday driving, at very reasonable prices.

Don't buy any 1978-81 Camaro with the expectation that it will explode later in value. The sleepers in this group, if they exist, will continue to snooze for quite a while.

Camaros have always held their value well—usually second only to Corvettes in the Chevrolet line—but the 1978-81 Camaros, particularly the 1980 and 1981 models, saw their values depressed by the stunning 1982 Camaro. Check that NADA guide for the price difference between 1982 and 1983 (not much), then 1982 and 1981 (much). The 1982 and later Camaros are worth every penny, but if the styling of the last of the second generation suits you, these are unquestionably among today's best values in the used-car market.

CHAPTER 10
1982-1987 Camaro

★★★

★★★ Z-28

★★★★ IROC-Z

★★★★ IROC-Z Convertible

1982 Model Production: 189,747
1983 Model Production: 154,381
1984 Model Production: 261,591
1985 Model Production: 180,018
1986 Model Production: 192,219

The third Camaro generation was ushered in by the 1982 model. It was a completely new Camaro but, just as with the transition from first generation to second, one with strong linkage to the Camaro heritage.

In 1975, Chevrolet began looking seriously at design themes for a new Camaro. It was assumed then that any start-from-scratch Camaro design would be front engine with front-wheel drive. Chevrolet purchased Volkswagen Sciroccos for evaluation, because components from GM's X-car program could have easily lent themselves to a Camaro along the lines of Volkswagen's sporty and fuel-efficient coupe.

Not everyone in the Chevrolet and Pontiac engineering groups was willing to depart from the front-engine, rear-drive configuration that had served the Camaro so well. Front-wheel-drive cars can be engineered to handle well, but having power delivery and steering at the same end can never quite equal the degree of control possible when power and steering are at opposite ends. This is especially true for amateur drivers who don't consider themselves amateur, and many Camaro owners fit that description.

There was also the issue of power. The necessity of dipping into the corporate parts bin for front-wheel-drive parts (or mid-engine parts, had the X components been relocated, a configuration briefly considered for the third Camaro generation) meant that six-cylinder engines would have been the largest possible. Chevrolet and Pontiac (especially Pontiac) felt the V-8 had many strong sales years left. So, in the interests of tradition, it was decided to make the new Camaro along the same front-engine, rear-drive layout as earlier Camaros, but to lighten and tighten the new body as much as possible.

The second generation of Camaros—those built between 1970 and 1981—wasn't an easy act to follow. Other than the Corvette, few Chevrolet products had such a long and mostly successful life. The designers' challenge was to maintain the Camaro identity, and still bring the car up to contemporary standards.

The third-generation Camaro has been an unprecedented success, one that's gained the admiration of the entire automotive world. The only complaints one hears are that the car is too big and space inefficient, or that there are just too many around. The first criticism is valid, the second mere testimony to the Camaro's broad appeal.

The third-generation Camaros are years away from being collector or investment cars, but they are destined to be legends. *Motor Trend* magazine's owner

Camaro IROC-Z, 1985. Author photos.

survey for the 1982 model found that a whopping 87.9 percent rated the handling excellent, and 91.6 percent said they bought it for its looks. So if the goal was to keep the best Camaro traditions alive in the third generation, it appears Chevrolet has done it.

Target weight reductions for the 1982 Camaro were not met, but it did come out nearly 500 pounds lighter than the 1981 model. Interestingly, if a weight plot is made for the Camaro's entire life cycle, it shows an almost steady pattern of weight gain through the 1981 model. The 1982 model returns to the starting point, just seventy pounds lighter than the first 1967 models.

Compared with the 1981 model, the 1982 Camaro was 9.8 inches shorter, had a seven-inch-shorter wheelbase, and had overhangs reduced 1.3 inches in front and 1.5 inches in the rear. It was 2.8 inches narrower, though the front wheel tread was down just a half inch, and the rear was 1.6 inches wider.

Less weight and fuel-economy requirements prompted Chevrolet to offer the 1982 Camaro with a four-cylinder engine. It was the Pontiac Iron Duke, an in-line four-cylinder (RPO LC1) with 151 cubic inches of displacement and 90 horsepower. The remaining 1982 Camaro engines were Chevrolet-made. The RPO LC1 was a V-6 with 173-cubic-inch displacement and 102 horsepower and served as the base Berlinetta powerplant. The standard Z-28 engine was the RPO LG4 with 305 cubic inches (five liters) and 145 horsepower. It had a single four-barrel carburetor. Another 305-cubic-inch engine, optional only with the Z-28, was the throttle-body-fuel-injected RPO LU5 with 165 horsepower. It came only with automatic transmission.

All engines were available in California with the same power ratings, but there were slight differences in transmission and axle availability. For instance, in California the V-6 couldn't be combined with the four-speed manual transmission.

The three Camaro base models for 1982 were neatly separated by mission. The Sport Coupe was the economy offering and had the four-cylinder engine as standard equipment. The Berlinetta was again the luxury car, and the Z-28 was the performance model. All were trimmed differently, with the Z-28 being recognized by its different front end (no upper grille openings) and lower side "ground-

---

1982-87 Camaro

BASE ENGINE (FOUR CYLINDER)*

Type: . . . . Inline ohv 4 (Pontiac build)
Bore x Stroke, inches: . . . . 4.00 × .00
Displacement, inches: 151
Compression Ratio: 8.25:1 (1982-83) 9.00:1 (1984-85)
Horsepower: . . . . 90 @ 4000 rpm
Torque: . . . . 134 @ 2400 rpm
Distributor: . . . . High energy ignition (breakerless)
Other engines: . . . *Four-cylinder was base for 1982-85, V-6 for 1986-87. V-6 and V-8 engines were available in displacements of 173-cid (V-6), 305-cid and 350-cid (V-8) with power ratings from 102-hp to 225-hp.

CHASSIS AND DRIVETRAIN

Clutch: . . . . Single dry-plate
Transmission: . . . Four-speed manual (1982-85), Five-speed manual (1986-87). Five-speed manual, three speed automatic and four-speed automatic optional
Front suspension: . . . . Modified MacPherson with struts and coil springs
Rear suspension: . . . . Torque arm with struts and coil springs
Axle ratio: . . . . 3.41:1 (others available)
Frame: . . . . Unibody with bolt-on front crossmember

GENERAL

Wheelbase, inches: 101.0
Height, inches: 49.8
Width, inches: 72.8
Length, inches: . . . . 187.8 (1982-84, 1985-87 non-Z), 192.0 (1985-87 Z28)
Brakes, standard: . . . . . . Disc front, drum rear, power assist
Wheels: . . . . Steel
Body material: . . . . Steel
Tire size, base: P195/75R-14
Fuel capacity, gallons: 16.2

effects" air dams. For clarity, let's review what each model consisted of by way of standard equipment.

The Sport Coupe, in addition to the four-cylinder engine, had power steering, power brakes (disc front, drum rear), reclining front bucket seats and a fold-down rear seat.

The Berlinetta Coupe, in addition to or in place of Sport Coupe equipment, had the V-6, aluminum wheels, custom seatbelts, deluxe luggage compartment, dual horns, P205/70R-14 steel-belted radial blackwall tires, quartz clock, quiet sound group, special instrumentation with tach, sport mirrors, two-tone paint, upgraded trim and moldings.

The Z-28, in addition to or in place of Sport Coupe equipment, had the RPO LG4 V-8 engine, aluminum wheels (different from the Berlinetta), leather-wrapped steering wheel, P215/65R-15 white-letter radial tires, rear spoiler, special instrumentation with tach, and additional upgraded trim and moldings.

The 1982 Camaro was all-new inside, with a very functional instrument panel. There was a glovebox in the console but none in the dash. Seats had always been a weak point of earlier Camaros, but those days were gone. All Camaros came with front bucket seats, and all had reclining mechanisms. The Conteur seat, built for Chevrolet by Lear-Siegler, was available for the driver and had six separate adjustments, including backrest bolster, thigh support, cushion bolster, lumbar and recliner. It was optional in the Z-28 and not cheap at $611.

In true Detroit tradition, the option list for the 1982 Camaro had grown a mile long again. But it wasn't a multitude of engines and transmissions that dominated as in the musclecar days. In 1982 Camaros, there were five different radios, with sixteen different radio and antenna prices, depending on which radio and antenna were combined with which Camaro model and trim level. You also

Chevrolet said its 1982 Z-28 was the "Total-performance Camaro. Its side-view mirrors as wind tunnel-tuned as its flared front air dam, is lighter by 500 pounds and leaner by almost three inches than its 1981 predecessor. Aerodynamic drag coefficient is .368. Functional cold-air inlets signify the presence of a Cross-Fire electronic fuel-injected 5.0-liter V8 engine under the hood. All 1982 Camaro models share a 101-inch wheelbase, MacPherson strut front suspension, and glass rear hatch." The beautiful five-spoke wheels were standard with the 1982 Z-28 and no others were available for it. The Cross-Fire injection motor (RPO LU5) was a Z-28 option at $450. Cross-Fire sales in 1982 were 24,673 out of 63,563 Z-28's sold. Chevrolet photos.

The fuel filler door moved to the driver's-side fender in 1982, a Camaro first. The license plate holder was hinged to reveal an external keyed hatch release. Author photos.

The 1982 Camaro instrument panel was new and a knockout for aesthetics and function, as were the door panel and console designs. The 1982 speedometer (and 1983-84) had an unusual double-pointer needle that simultaneously indicated miles-per-hour and kilometers-per-hour on separate scales. The four-position rocker switch at the forward edge of the door panel console controlled the RPO DG7 electric remote mirrors. They cost $89 extra with the Z-28 and 18,232 were sold in 1982. Author photos.

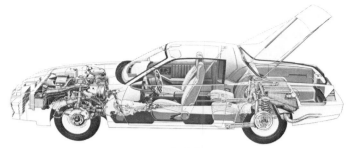

1982 Camaro. Chevrolet illustration.

1982 Camaro Colors/Options

Color Code	Body Color
11	White
16	Silver
19	Black
21	Light Blue
29	Dark Blue
45	Light Jade
49	Dark Jade
55	Gold
67	Dark Gold
75	Red
78	Maroon
84	Charcoal

INTERIOR COLORS: Dark Blue, Camel, Charcoal, Jade, Maroon, Silver Gray

Order #	Item Description	Sticker $
1FP87	Camaro Sport Coupe	8,029.50
1FS87	Camaro Berlinetta Coupe	9,665.06
1FP87	Z28 Camaro Sport Coupe	10,099.26
1FP87	Z28/Z50 Camaro Indy 500 Edition	10,999.26
AG9	Power Seat, Driver's Side	197.00
AU3	Door Lock System, Power	106.00
A01	Glass, Tinted	88.00
A31	Power Windows	165.00
A90	Power Hatch Release	32.00
BS1	Quiet Sound Group (w/Sp Cpe)	82.00
BS1	Quiet Sound Group (w/Z28)	72.00
BX5	Moldings, Roof Drip, Black	29.00
B32	Mats, Color-Keyed Floor, Front	16.00
B33	Mats, Color-Keyed Floor, Rear	11.00
B48	Luggage Compartment Trim, Deluxe	164.00
B84	Moldings, Body Side	47.00
B93	Moldings, Door Edge	15.00
CC1	Roof Panels, Removable Glass	790.00
CD4	Windshield Wipers, Intermittent	47.00
C25	Rear Window Wiper/Washer	117.00
C49	Defogger, Rear Window Electric	125.00
C60	Air Conditioning	675.00
DG7	Mirrors, Electric Remote (w/Sp Cpe)	137.00
DG7	Mirrors, Electric Remote (w/Z28 & Berl)	89.00
D35	Mirrors, Sport (std w/Z28 & Berl)	48.00
D80	Spoiler, Rear (std w/Z28)	69.00
F41	Suspension, Sport	49.00
G80	Axle, Limited Slip	76.48
G92	Axle, Performance Ratio	21.00
J65	Brakes, Power Disc Front & Rear	179.00
K35	Cruise Control w/Resume (w/MX1)	155.00
K35	Cruise Control w/Resume (w/o MX1)	165.00
LC1	Engine, 102-hp, 173-cid V-6	125.00

Order #	Item Description	Sticker $
LG4	Engine, 145-hp, 305-cid V-8 (w/Sp Cpe)	295.00
LG4	Engine, 145-hp, 305-cid V-8 (w/Berl)	170.00
LU5	Engine, 165-hp, 305-cid V-8 (Z28 only)	450.00
MM4	Transmission, 4-Speed	n/c
MX1	Transmission, Automatic	396.00
MX1	Transmission, Automatic (w/Z28)	72.00
N33	Steering Wheel, Comfortilt	95.00
PO1	Full Wheel Covers	52.00
QVJ	Tires, P195/75R-14 WW (w/Sp Cpe)	126.60
QVU	Tires, P205/70R-14 WW (w/Berl)	66.00
QVU	Tires, P205/70R-14 WW (w/Sp Cpe)	188.56
QXV	Tires, P195/75R-14 3W (w/Sp Cpe)	64.60
QYA	Tires, P205/70R-14 BW (w/Sp Cpe)	122.56
QYC	Tires, P205/70R-14 Ltr (w/Sp Cpe)	210.56
QYG	Tires, P195/75R-14 WW (w/Sp Cpe)	62.00
TR9	Lighting, Auxiliary	52.00
TT5	Halogen Headlights, Highbeam	10.00
UA1	Battery, Heavy-Duty	25.00
UE8	Clock, Digital (w/Sp Cpe)	60.00
UE8	Clock, Digital (w/Z28 & Berl)	28.00
U05	Horns, Dual	12.00
U21	Instrumentation, Special	149.00
U35	Clock, Quartz Electric (w/Sp Cpe)	32.00
U63	Radio, AM	111.00
U69	Radio, AM-FM	172.00
U73	Antenna, Fixed Mast (incl w/radios)	41.00
U75	Antenna, Power	55.00
U81	Speakers, Dual Rear (w/Cust, Berl)	30.00
U81	Speakers, Dual Rear (w/o Cust)	54.00
V08	Cooling, Heavy-Duty (w/o C60)	70.00
V08	Cooling, Heavy-Duty (w/C60)	40.00
YE1	AM-FM Stereo (w/o Cust)	282.00
YE1	AM-FM Stereo (w/Cust, Berl)	258.00
YE3	AM-FM St, 8-trk (Z28 w/o Cust)	414.00
YE3	AM-FM St, 8-trk (Z28 & Berl w/Cust)	390.00
YE3	AM-FM St, 8-trk (Sp Cpe w/Cust)	422.00
YE3	AM-FM St, 8-trk (Sp Cpe w/o Cust)	417.00
YE4	AM-FM St, Cass (Z28 w/o Cust)	409.00
YE4	AM-FM St, Cass (Z28 & Berl w/Cust)	385.00
YE4	AM-FM St, Cass (Sp Cpe w/Cust)	417.00
YE4	AM-FM St, Cass (Sp Cpe w/o Cust)	441.00
ZJ7	Wheel Trim, Rally Wheels	112.00
C--2	Cloth Seats	28.00
C--9	Sport Cloth LS Conteur Seats (w/Z28)	312.00
F--9	Custom Cloth Seats (w/Sp Cpe, Z28)	299.00
F--9	Custom Cloth LS Conteur Seats (w/Z28)	611.00
X--2	Custom Vinyl Seats (w/Sp Cpe, Z28)	299.00

• Prices shown were introductory retail.

For the third time in its history, Camaro paced the Indianapolis 500 race in 1982. Chevrolet sold 6,360 Camaro Pace Car replicas to the public. Here's how Chevrolet introduced the 1982 Pace Car to the motoring press on May 1, 1982:

"DETROIT — Six thousand 'Commemorative Edition' Camaro Z28s sporting the dynamite graphics and special interior of the Indy 500 pace car are being produced for sale through Chevrolet dealers.

'Commemorative Edition' vehicles are all Z28s with exclusive silver and blue exteriors, Indy 500 accents and logos, sport mirrors and red-accent silver aluminum wheels with white-lettered Goodyear Eagle GT tires.

Inside, the cars are all equipped with special instrumentation, AM/FM stereo, a leather-wrapped steering wheel, deluxe luggage compartment trim and a blue cloth and silver vinyl interior that features Camaro's exclusive adjustable L/S Conteur driver's seat.

All 'Commemorative Edition' Z28s are being built at GM's Van Nuys, California assembly plant. The first cars came off the assembly line in early March. The last will be built in mid-April.

Chevrolet dealers, who were offered opportunities to order one 'Commemorative Edition' apiece for delivery in early May, could select a carbureted or fuel injected 5.0-liter V8 engine, and either automatic or manual transmission.

A lengthy option list includes removable glass T tops, air conditioning, four-wheel disc brakes and tinted glass." Chevrolet photos.

146

had seven tire choices in the fourteen-inch size, though the Z-28 came with one fifteen-inch-style tire only.

Transmission choice was limited to four-speed manuals and three-speed automatics. Three-speed manuals had been in the base units up until 1981, but they were gone for the third generation.

All 1982 Camaros had power brakes with discs in front and drums in back. Four-wheel disc brakes were optional (RPO J65) with any V-8 Camaro for $179. For the first time in Camaro history, a six-way power seat could be ordered. Along with the usual power windows and power door locks, there was an optional power release for the rear hatch. A washer and wiper could be purchased for the hatch, too.

Windshield antennas weren't part of the third generation, but there was a choice of body-mounted fixed or power antennas. All but the RPO U63 AM radio and RPO U69 AM-FM radio came with a premium speaker arrangement Chevrolet called ERS (Extended Range Sound). Removable glass roof panels were optional with the 1982 Camaro as RPO CC1 for $790.

For the third time, the Camaro was honored with selection as Pace Car for the 1982 Indianapolis 500 race. The actual Pace Car and one backup were built at the Van Nuys Camaro plant in California, as were 6,360 replicas for sale to the public. All were silver-and-blue Z-28's with Indy 500 accents and decals, sport mirrors and red-accented silver aluminum wheels with white-letter Goodyear Eagle GT tires. Inside, they had special instrumentation, AM-FM stereo radio, leather-wrapped steering wheel, deluxe luggage compartment trim and a blue-cloth-and-silver-vinyl interior with the Lear-Siegler Conteur driver's seat. Replicas could have either of the V-8's available in all Z-28's, but the actual Pace Cars for the race were fitted with aluminum-block 350-cubic-inch engines with 250 horsepower. Suspensions for the Pace Cars and the replicas were stock Z-28.

The 1982 Camaro was selected as *Motor Trend* magazine's Car of the Year. The 1982 model year was a short one for the Camaro because of its February introduction, but sales were fantastic at 189,747 units. It was the hottest-selling car in Chevrolet's stable for the period. The 1983 didn't need major changes, and it didn't get them.

There were some 1983 revisions in the engine and transmission areas. In April 1983, a new 305-cubic-inch V-8 option for the Z-28 was released. It had a different camshaft, Rochester four-barrel carburetor, and delivered an impressive 190 horsepower. It was RPO L69, but it became known as the five-liter HO (high output). At $450, the extra cost of the RPO L69 equaled the throttle-body-injected RPO LU5, but the new engine made twenty-five more horsepower, and did it with less-exotic hardware. Needless to say, the new engine became a hit, and the throttle-body-injected (TBI) version departed from the 1984 order sheets.

There were other minor option changes for the 1983 model. A rear compartment cover (RPO D42) hid valuables from view through the huge rear window. It cost $64. Optional floormats became carpeted instead of rubber.

The third-generation Camaro became another Chevrolet success story, confirmed by sales of 154,381 in the 1983 model year. So again, no major changes were needed for 1984.

Since the Z-28 was gathering all the accolades, Chevrolet decided to invest more effort in the Berlinetta. For 1984, the Berlinetta got a space-age electronic instrument cluster unique to it. The new layout featured a digital readout for

1983 Z28. Chevrolet photo.

1983 Camaro Colors/Options

Color Code	Body Color
11	White
15	Silver
19	Black
22	Light Blue
27	Dark Blue
59	Beige
62	Light Brown
65	Dark Gold
67	Dark Brown
75	Red
82	Charcoal

INTERIOR COLORS: Charcoal, Charcoal/Burnt Orange, Dark Blue, Camel, Sand Gray, Dark Brown

Order #	Item Description	Sticker $
1FP87	Camaro Sport Coupe	8,036.00
1FS87	Camaro Berlinetta Coupe	9,881.00
1FP87	Z28 Camaro Sport Coupe	10,336.00
AG9	Power Seat, Driver's Side	210.00
AU3	Door Lock System, Power	120.00
A01	Glass, Tinted	105.00
A31	Power Windows	180.00
A90	Power Hatch Release	40.00
BS1	Quiet Sound Group (w/Sp Cpe)	82.00
BS1	Quiet Sound Group (w/Z28)	72.00
BX5	Moldings, Roof Drip	29.00
B34	Mats, Front Carpeted	20.00
B35	Mats, Rear Carpeted	15.00
B48	Luggage Compartment Trim, Deluxe	164.00
B84	Moldings, Body Side	55.00
B93	Moldings, Door Edge	15.00
CC1	Roof Panels, Removable Glass	825.00
CD4	Windshield Wipers, Intermittent	49.00
C25	Rear Window Wiper/Washer	120.00
C49	Defogger, Rear Window Electric	135.00
C60	Air Conditioning	725.00
DG7	Mirrors, Electric Remote (w/Sp Cpe)	137.00
DG7	Mirrors, Electric Remote (w/Z28 & Berl)	89.00
D35	Mirrors, Sport (std w/Z28 & Berl)	51.00
D42	Cover, Rear Compartment	64.00
D80	Spoiler, Rear (std w/Z28)	69.00
F41	Suspension, Sport	49.00
G80	Axle, Limited Slip	95.47
G92	Axle, Performance Ratio	21.00
J65	Brakes, Power Disc Front & Rear	179.00
K35	Cruise Control w/Resume	170.00
LC1	Engine, 107-hp, 173-cid V-6	150.00
LG4	Engine, 150-hp, 305-cid V-8 (w/Sp Cpe)	350.00
LG4	Engine, 150-hp, 305-cid V-8 (w/Berl)	225.00

Order #	Item Description	Sticker $
LU5	Engine, 175-hp, 305-cid V-8 (Z28 only)	450.00
L69	Engine, 190-hp, 305-cid V-8 (Z28 only)	450.00
MM4	Transmission, 4-Speed (w/Sp Cpe)	n/c
MM5	Transmission, 5-Speed (w/Sp Cpe)	125.00
MX1	Transmission, Automatic (w/Sp Cpe)	425.00
MX1	Transmission, Automatic (w/Berl)	195.00
MX0	Transmission, Automatic (w/Sp Cpe)	525.00
MX0	Transmission, Automatic (w/Z28, Berl)	295.00
N33	Steering Wheel, Comfortilt	105.00
P01	Full Wheel Covers	52.00
QVJ	Tires, P195/75R-14 WW (w/Sp Cpe)	126.48
QVU	Tires, P205/70R-14 WW (w/Berl)	66.00
QVU	Tires, P205/70R-14 WW (w/Sp Cpe)	188.68
QXV	Tires, P195/75R-14 BW (w/Sp Cpe)	64.48
QYA	Tires, P205/70R-14 BW (w/Sp Cpe)	122.08
QYC	Tires, P205/70R-14 Ltr (w/Sp Cpe)	210.68
QYG	Tires, P195/75R-14 WW (w/Sp Cpe)	62.00
TR9	Lighting, Auxiliary	52.00
TT5	Halogen Headlights, Highbeam	10.00
UA1	Battery, Heavy-Duty	25.00
UE8	Clock, Digital (w/Sp Cpe)	39.00
UE8	Clock, Digital (w/Z28, Berl)	n/c
UO5	Horns, Dual	12.00
U21	Instrumentation, Special	149.00
U35	Clock, Quartz Electric (w/Sp Cpe)	35.00
U63	Radio, AM	112.00
U69	Radio, AM-FM	171.00
U73	Antenna, Fixed Mast (incl w/radios)	41.00
U75	Antenna, Power	60.00
U81	Speakers, Dual Rear	30.00
V08	Cooling, Heavy-Duty (w/o C60)	70.00
V08	Cooling, Heavy-Duty (w/C60)	40.00
YE1	AM-FM Stereo (w/Sp Cpe)	302.00
YE1	AM-FM Stereo (w/Z28, Berl)	267.00
YE2	AM-FM St, Cass, SS, Clk (w/Sp Cpe)	555.00
YE2	AM-FM St, Cass, SS, Clk (w/Z28, Berl)	520.00
YE4	AM-FM St, Cass, Clk (w/Sp Cpe)	402.00
YE4	AM-FM St, Cass, Clk (w/Z28)	367.00
YF1	AM-FM Stereo	263.00
ZJ7	Wheel Trim, Rally Wheels	112.00
C--2	Cloth Seats	28.00
C--9	Sport Cloth LS Conteur Seats (w/Z28)	375.00
F--2	Custom Cloth Seats (w/Sp Cpe)	299.00
F--2	Custom Cloth Seats (w/Z28)	227.00
F--9	Custom Cloth LS Conteur Seats (w/Z28)	650.00
X--2	Custom Vinyl Seats (w/Sp Cpe)	299.00
X--2	Custom Vinyl Seats (w/Z28)	227.00

• Prices shown were introductory retail.

speed, an electronic "thermometer" display for engine revolutions, and more. Here's the way Chevrolet put it in its 1984 Camaro dealer brochure: "Much has been made of bringing aircraft-type precision ergonomics to today's cars. Berlinetta is at the very forefront of this concept with dual sliding computer terminals that position the car's key driving, visibility and comfort controls a fingertip away from the steering wheel. This system may be expanded to include the available electronic speed control with resume speed feature that you also may program to increase or decrease speed in precise increments. And mounted just beyond the standard five-speed gearshift, there's a standard remote-control, electronically tuned AM-FM stereo radio with seek and scan, clock and Extended Range Sound system (ERS). It swivels for easy operation by driver or passenger. You'll find its audio performance and stunning design perfectly complement Berlinetta's beautifully isolated, acoustically superb interior."

The Z-28 gathered the accolades when the third generation appeared, and for good reason. But in 1984, Chevrolet invested some attention in the Berlinetta and gave it this "star wars" instrument panel. Magazine writers thought it a little much, but it made sense for the Berlinetta's high-tech luxury mission. Chevrolet photos.

If that wasn't enough, the Berlinetta also came with a roof console that held a map light that swiveled, a removable flashlight, mileage reminder spools and a cute little pouch for sunglasses or garage door opener. The roof console was available on non-Berlinetta Camaros for $50.

Road & Track picked the 1984 Camaro as one of the world's twelve best en-

1984 Camaro Colors/Options

Color Code	Body Color
11	White
15	Silver
19	Black
22	Light Blue
27	Dark Blue
59	Beige
62	Light Brown
65	Dark Gold
67	Dark Brown
75	Red
82	Charcoal

INTERIOR COLORS: Dark Blue, Dark Brown, Camel, Charcoal, Charcoal/Red, Sand Gray

Order #	Item Description	Sticker $
1FP87	Camaro Sport Coupe	8,409.00
1FS87	Camaro Berlinetta Coupe	11,309.00
1FP87	Z28 Camaro Sport Coupe	11,034.00
AG9	Power Seat, Driver's Side	215.00
AU3	Door Lock System, Power	125.00
A01	Glass, Tinted	110.00
A31	Power Windows	185.00
A90	Power Hatch Release	40.00
BS1	Quiet Sound Group (w/Sp Cpe)	82.00
BS1	Quiet Sound Group (w/Z28)	72.00
BX5	Moldings, Roof Drip	29.00
B34	Mats, Front Carpeted	20.00
B35	Mats, Rear Carpeted	15.00
B48	Luggage Compt Trim (w/Sp Cpe)	164.00
B48	Luggage Compt Trim (w/Z28)	84.00
B84	Moldings, Body Side	55.00
B91	Moldings, Door Edge Guard, Black	15.00
CC1	Roof Panels, Removable Glass	825.00
CD4	Windshield Wipers, Intermittent	50.00
C25	Rear Window Wiper/Washer	120.00
C49	Defogger, Rear Window Electric	140.00
C60	Air Conditioning	730.00
C67	Air Cond, Electronic Control (w/Berl)	730.00
DG7	Mirrors, Electric Remote (w/Sp Cpe)	139.00
DG7	Mirrors, Electric Remote (w/Z28, Berl)	91.00
DK6	Console, Interior Roof	50.00
D27	Cover, Locking Rear Floor Storage	80.00
D35	Mirrors, Sport (std w/Z28 & Berl)	53.00
D42	Cover, Rear Compartment	69.00
D80	Spoiler, Rear (std w/Z28)	69.00
F41	Suspension, Sport	49.00
G80	Axle, Limited Slip	95.53
G92	Axle, Performance Ratio (w/Z28)	21.00
J65	Brakes, Power Disc Front and Rear	179.00
K05	Heater, Engine Block	20.00
K34	Cruise Control w/Resume (w/Sp Cpe, Z28)	175.00
K34	Cruise Control w/Resume (w/Berl)	185.00

Order #	Item Description	Sticker $
LC1	Engine, 107-hp, 173-cid V-6	250.00
LG4	Engine, 150-hp, 305-cid V-8 (w/Sp Cpe)	550.00
LG4	Engine, 150-hp, 305-cid V-8 (w/Berl)	375.00
L69	Engine, 180-hp, 305-cid V-8 (w/Z28)	530.00
MM4	Transmission, 4-Speed (w/Sp Cpe)	n/c
MM5	Transmission, 5-Speed (w/Sp Cpe)	125.00
MX0	Transmission, Automatic (w/Sp Cpe)	525.00
MX0	Transmission, Automatic (w/Z28, Berl)	295.00
N33	Steering Wheel, Comfortilt	110.00
P01	Full Wheel Covers	52.00
QHW	Tires, P205/70R-14 Ltr (w/Sp Cpe)	146.44
QHX	Tires, P205/70R-14 BW (w/Sp Cpe)	58.44
QHY	Tires, P205/70R-14 WW (w/Berl)	66.00
QHY	Tires, P205/70R-14 WW (w/Sp Cpe)	124.44
QMX	Tires, P195/75R-14 WW (w/Sp Cpe)	62.00
QYZ	Tires, P215/65R-15 BW (w/Z28-LS9)	−92.00
TR9	Lighting, Aux (Sp Cpe & Z28 w/o DK6)	72.00
TR9	Lighting, Aux (Sp Cpe & Z28 w/DK6)	48.00
TR9	Lighting, Aux (w/Berl)	37.00
TT5	Halogen Headlights, Highbeam	10.00
UA1	Battery, Heavy-Duty	26.00
UL5	Radio Delete (Berl only)	−331.00
U05	Horns, Dual	12.00
UT4	AM-FM St, Cass, SS, Clk, EQ (w/Berl)	203.00
U21	Instrumentation, Special	149.00
U35	Clock, Quartz Electric (w/Sp Cpe)	35.00
U63	Radio, AM	112.00
U69	Radio, AM-FM	171.00
U73	Antenna, Fixed Mast (incl w/radios)	41.00
U75	Antenna, Power	60.00
U81	Speakers, Dual Rear	30.00
V08	Cooling, Heavy-Duty (w/o C60 or C67)	70.00
V08	Cooling, Heavy-Duty (w/C60 or C67)	40.00
YE1	AM-FM St, Clk (w/Sp Cpe)	302.00
YE1	AM-FM St, Clk (w/Z28, Berl)	267.00
YE2	AM-FM St, Cass, SS, Clk, EQ (w/Sp Cpe)	605.00
YE2	AM-FM St, Cass, SS, Clk, EQ (w/Z28)	570.00
YE4	AM-FM St, Cass, Clk (w/Sp Cpe)	402.00
YE4	AM-FM St, Cass, Clk (w/Z28)	367.00
YF1	AM-FM Stereo	263.00
YF5	Emission Equipment, California	99.00
ZJ7	Wheel Trim, Rally Wheels	112.00
C--2	Cloth Seats	28.00
C--9	Sport Cloth LS Conteur Seats (w/Z28)	375.00
F--2	Custom Cloth Seats (w/Sp Cpe)	359.00
F--2	Custom Cloth Seats (w/Z28)	287.00
F--9	Custom Cloth LS Conteur Seats (w/Z28)	650.00
X--2	Custom Vinyl Seats (w/Sp Cpe)	359.00
X--2	Custom Vinyl Seats (w/Z28)	287.00

• Prices shown were introductory retail.

thusiast cars. It (along with the Trans Am) won the Best Sports GT category in the $11,000-$14,000 range. As the magazine put it, "Beneath the skin lies a strong thumping heart—a 5.0 liter High Output V-8 engine that boasts 190-horsepower and 240 lb-ft torque. Power is delivered to the rear wheels via a beefy five-speed manual (or optional four-speed automatic). Inside, both the Pontiac and the Chevrolet present a driver's compartment with a distinctive, high-tech look about it, with plenty of large, easy-to-read gauges. Space efficiency is not terribly good, however, and the rear seat is only marginally useful. But if your taste in cars runs to powerful V-8's with abundant torque, a manly gearbox and high handling limits, the Camaro Z-28 or Firebird Trans Am will knock you out."

For its part, *Car and Driver* did a cover story article in its May 1984 issue searching for "America's best handling car." The cover showed a red Corvette at speed. But surprise! When the numbers were added, it was the Camaro, at little more than half the Corvette's price, on top.

Chevrolet introduced a hot new Z-28 option for 1985 called the IROC-Z. Named after the International Race of Champions (an annual four-event series for top drivers from different kinds of racing, all using identically-prepared Camaros), the street-version IROC Camaro featured lower trim height and center

Big news for 1985 included the IROC-Z and new Tuned-Port fuel-injected engine (RPO LB9). But these didn't necessarily go together. The IROC-Z wasn't a separate model, it was an option (RPO B4Z) for the Z-28. Both the regular Z-28 and one with the IROC package came with the RPO LG4 as the base V-8. Initially at least, both could be upgraded to the Tuned-Port engine, but only with an automatic transmission. The RPO L69 HO engine cost $680 just like the Tuned-Port, but the high-output V-8 came only with a manual five-speed and could only be mated with an IROC-Z. Chevrolet photo.

of gravity; special front struts, springs and jounce bumpers; Delco-Bilstein rear shocks; special rear springs and stabilizer bar; higher-effort steering; increased caster; front-wheel alignment; front frame rail reinforcement; 16x8-inch aluminum wheels; Goodyear Eagle P245/50VR sixteen-inch blackwall tires; and unique exterior graphics. All this added up to a Camaro that could pull 0.92 g's on the skid pad and seven-second 0-60 times—all in showroom trim. The IROC-Z could be ordered with either a carbureted RPO L69 V-8, or with a new RPO

1985 Camaro Colors/Options

Color Code	Body Color
11	White
12	Silver
15	Medium Gray
19	Black
26	Dark Blue
30	Bright Blue
50	Yellow
54	Light Yellow
60	Light Brown
69	Copper
75	Red
78	Maroon

INTERIOR COLORS: Black, Copper, Gray, Red, Saddle

Order #	Item Description	Sticker $
1FP87	Camaro Sport Coupe	8,777.00
1FS87	Camaro Berlinetta Coupe	11,474.00
1FP87	Z28 Camaro Sport Coupe	11,474.00
AG9	Power Seat, Driver's Side	215.00
AM9	Seat Back, Split Folding Rear	50.00
AU3	Door Lock System, Power	125.00
A01	Glass, Tinted	110.00
A31	Power Windows	185.00
A90	Power Hatch Release	40.00
BS1	Quiet Sound Group	82.00
BX5	Moldings, Roof Drip	29.00
B4Z	Sport Equipment Package, I.R.O.C.	659.00
B34	Mats, Front Carpeted	20.00
B35	Mats, Rear Carpeted	15.00
B48	Luggage Compt Trim (w/Sp Cpe)	164.00
B48	Luggage Compt Trim (w/Z28)	84.00
B84	Moldings, Body Side, Black	55.00
B91	Moldings, Door Edge Guard, Black	15.00
CC1	Roof Panels, Removable Glass	821.00
CD4	Windshield wipers, Intermittent	50.00
C25	Rear Window Wiper/Washer	120.00
C49	Defogger, Rear Window Electric	140.00
C60	Air Conditioning	730.00
C67	Air Cond, Electronic Control (w/Berl)	730.00
DG7	Mirrors, Electric Remote (w/Sp Cpe)	139.00
DG7	Mirrors, Electric Remote (w/Z28, Berl)	91.00
DK6	Console, Interior Roof	50.00
D27	Cover, Locking Rear Floor Storage	80.00
D35	Mirrors, Sport (std w/Z28 & Berl)	53.00
D42	Cover, Rear Compartment	69.00
D80	Spoiler, Rear (std w/Z28)	69.00
F41	Suspension, Sport	49.00
G80	Axle, Limited Slip	95.00
J65	Brakes, Power Disc Front and Rear	179.00
K05	Heater, Engine Block	20.00

IROC →

Order #	Item Description	Sticker $
K34	Cruise Control w/Resume (w/Sp Cpe, Z28)	175.00
K34	Cruise Control w/Resume (w/Berl)	185.00
LB8	Engine, 135-hp, 173-cid V-6	335.00
LB9	Engine, 215-hp, 305-cid V-8	680.00
LG4	Engine, 155-hp, 305-cid V-8 (w/Sp Cpe)	635.00
LG4	Engine, 155-hp, 305-cid V-8 (w/Berl)	300.00
L69	Engine, 190-hp, 305-cid V-8 (w/Z28)	680.00
MM5	Transmission, 5-Speed	n/c
MX0	Transmission, Automatic	395.00
N33	Steering Wheel, Comfortilt	110.00
N90	Wheels, Aluminum	225.00
P01	Full Wheel Covers	52.00
QAC	Tires, P235/60R-15 BW (w/Z28)	85.00
QHW	Tires, P205/70R-14 Ltr (w/Sp Cpe)	146.00
QHX	Tires, P205/70R-14 BW (w/Sp Cpe)	58.00
QHY	Tires, P205/70R-14 WW (w/Berl)	66.00
QHY	Tires, P205/70R-14 WW (w/Sp Cpe)	124.00
QMX	Tires, P195/75R-14 WW (w/Sp Cpe)	62.00
TR9	Lighting, Aux (Sp Cpe & Z28 w/o DK6)	72.00
TR9	Lighting, Aux (Sp Cpe & Z28 w/DK6)	48.00
TR9	Lighting, Aux (w/Berl)	37.00
TT4	Halogen Headlights, High & Low Beam	22.00
UA1	Battery, Heavy-Duty	26.00
UL5	Radio Delete (w/Berl)	−256.00
UL5	Radio Delete (w/Z28, Sp Cpe)	−56.00
U05	Horns, Dual	12.00
UT4	AM-FM St, Cass, SS, Clk, EQ (w/Berl)	242.00
U21	Instrumentation, Special	149.00
U35	Clock, Quartz Electric (w/Sp Cpe)	35.00
U63	Radio, AM	112.00
U64	Speakers, Dual Rear	30.00
U69	Radio, AM-FM	82.00
U75	Antenna, Power	60.00
V08	Cooling, Heavy-Duty (w/o C60 or C67)	70.00
V08	Cooling, Heavy-Duty (w/C60 or C67)	40.00
YE1	AM-FM St, Clk (w/Sp Cpe)	212.00
YE1	AM-FM St, Clk (w/Z28)	177.00
YE2	AM-FM St, Cass, SS, Clk, EQ (w/Sp Cpe)	504.00
YE2	AM-FM St, Cass, SS, Clk, EQ (w/Z28)	469.00
YE3	AM-FM St, Cass, SS, Clk (w/Sp Cpe)	354.00
YE3	AM-FM St, Cass, SS, Clk (w/Z28)	319.00
YF1	AM-FM Stereo	173.00
YF5	Emission Equipment, California	99.00
ZJ7	Wheel Trim, Rally Wheel	112.00
C--2	Cloth Seats	28.00
F--2	Custom Cloth Seats (w/Sp Cpe, Z28)	359.00
F--9	Custom Cloth LS Contour Seats (w/Z28)	650.00

• Prices shown were introductory retail.

LB9 V-8 with port fuel injection. At introduction, the L69 motor could be linked with only the five-speed manual transmission, not the four-speed automatic. But the injected V-8 came initially only with the automatic because it developed too much torque for the manual transmission to handle.

The Berlinetta continued in 1985 with the Star Wars instrumentation introduced in 1984, but the rest of the Camaro lineup featured redesigned instrument faces. There were other detail refinements for all Camaros, like "wet arm"

1986 Camaro Colors/Options

Color Code	Body Color
13	Silver
23	Bright Blue
28	Dark Blue
40	White
41	Black
51	Yellow
60	Light Brown
66	Copper
68	Dark Brown
74	Dark Red
81	Bright Red
84	Medium Gray

INTERIOR COLORS: Black, Copper, Gray, Red, Saddle

Order #	Item Description	Sticker $
1FP87	Camaro Sport Coupe	9,349.00
1FS87	Camaro Berlinetta Coupe	12,316.00
1FP87	Z28 Camaro Sport Coupe	12,316.00
AG9	Power Seat, Driver's Side	225.00
AM9	Seat Back, Split Folding Rear	50.00
AU3	Door Lock System, Power	130.00
A01	Glass, Tinted	115.00
A31	Power Windows	195.00
A90	Power Hatch Release	40.00
BS1	Quiet Sound Group	82.00
B4K	AM-FM St, SS, Clk (w/Sp Cpe)	232.00
B4N	AM-FM St, SS	193.00
B4N	AM-FM St, SS, Clk (w/Z28)	197.00
B4Z	Sport Equipment Package, I.R.O.C.	659.00
B34	Mats, Front Carpeted	20.00
B35	Mats, Rear Carpeted	15.00
B48	Luggage Compt Trim (w/Sp Cpe)	164.00
B48	Luggage Compt Trim (w/Z28)	84.00
B84	Moldings, Body Side	55.00
B91	Moldings, Door Edge, Black	15.00
CC1	Roof Panels, Removable Glass	846.00
CD4	Windshield Wipers, Intermittent	50.00
C25	Rear Window Wiper/Washer	125.00
C49	Defogger, Rear Window Electric	145.00
C60	Air Conditioning	750.00
C67	Air Cond, Electronic Control (w/Berl)	750.00
DD8	Mirror, Inside Rearview Automatic	80.00
DE1	Louvers, Rear Window	210.00
DG7	Mirrors, Electric Remote	91.00
DK6	Console, Interior Roof	50.00
D27	Cover, Locking Rear Floor Storage	80.00
D42	Cover, Rear Compartment	69.00
D80	Spoiler, Rear (std w/Z28)	69.00
G80	Axle, Limited Slip	100.00

Order #	Item Description	Sticker $
G92	Axle, Performance Ratio (Z28)	21.00
J65	Brakes, Power Disc Front and Rear	179.00
K05	Heater, Engine Block	20.00
K34	Cruise Control w/Resume (w/Sp Cpe, Z28)	175.00
K34	Cruise Control w/Resume (w/Berl)	185.00
LB8	Engine, 135-hp, 173-cid V-6	350.00
LB9	Engine, 190-hp, 305-cid V-8 (w/Z28)	695.00
LG4	Engine, 155-hp, 305-cid V-8 (w/Sp Cpe)	750.00
LG4	Engine, 155-hp, 305-cid V-8 (w/Berl)	400.00
L69	Engine, 190-hp, 305-cid V-8 (w/Z28)	695.00
MM5	Transmission, 5-speed	n/c
MX0	Transmission, Automatic	465.00
N33	Steering Wheel, Comfortilt	115.00
PB4	Wheel Locking Package	16.00
QAC	Tires, P235/60R-15 BW (w/Z28)	85.00
QDX	Tires, P195/70R-14 BW (w/Berl)	80.00
QHX	Tires, P205/70R-14 BW (w/Berl)	n/c
QHY	Tires, P205/70R-14 WW (w/Berl)	66.00
QYH	Tires, P215/65R-15 Ltr (w/Sp Cpe)	92.00
QYH	Tires, P215/65R-15 Ltr (w/Z28)	n/c
QYZ	Tires, P215/65R-15 BW (w/Sp Cpe)	n/c
QYZ	Tires, P215/65R-15 BW (w/Z28)	-92.00
TR9	Lighting, Aux (Sp Cpe & Z28 w/o DK6)	72.00
TR9	Lighting, Aux (Sp Cpe & Z28 w/DK6)	48.00
TR9	Lighting, Aux (w/Berl)	37.00
TT4	Halogen Headlights, High & Low Beam	25.00
T96	Halogen Fog Lamps	60.00
UA1	Battery, Heavy-Duty	26.00
UL5	Radio Delete (w/Sp Cpe)	-56.00
UL5	Radio Delete (w/Berl)	-256.00
UL5	Radio Delete (w/Z28)	-95.00
UL6	Radio, AM, Clock (w/Sp Cpe)	39.00
UL6	Radio, AM, Clock (w/Z28)	n/c
UT4	AM-FM St, Cass, SS, Clk, EQ (w/Berl)	242.00
U05	Horns, Dual	12.00
U21	Instrumentation, Special	149.00
U75	Antenna, Power	65.00
V08	Cooling, Heavy-Duty (w/o C60 or C67)	70.00
V08	Cooling, Heavy-Duty (w/C60 or C67)	40.00
YE2	AM-FM St, Cass, SS, Clk, EQ (w/Sp Cpe)	504.00
YE2	AM-FM St, Cass, SS, Clk, EQ (w/Z28)	469.00
YE3	AM-FM St, Cass, SS, Clk (w/Sp Cpe)	354.00
YE3	AM-FM St, Cass, SS, Clk (w/Z28)	319.00
YF5	Emission Equipment, California	99.00
PE1	Wheels, Cast Aluminum (w/Berl)	225.00
C—2	Cloth Seats	28.00
F—2	Custom Cloth Seats (w/Sp Cpe, Z28)	359.00

• Prices shown were introductory retail.

windshield wipers (the washer squirters were mounted on the blades) and tweaked suspension bushings, spring rates and shock valving.

Speaking of the Berlinetta, it was discontinued a few months into 1986 production. Its soft suspension and dazzling electronic instrument panel were intended to entice luxury-minded customers into the Camaro fold, but the Berlinetta model just wasn't overly successful. It accounted for only thirteen-percent of Camaro sales in 1984 and 1985. In 1986, just 4,479 were sold.

The Camaro's engine bay saw some changes in 1986. The RPO LQ9 four-cylinder engine was officially the base powerplant, but Chevrolet records indicate none were installed. All 1986 and 1987 Camaros had V-6 or V-8 power. The RPO L69 High Output V-8 was also listed as an available option for Z28 models, but it too was generally unavailable, though records do show 74 were sold in 1986 Camaros. The RPO LB9 V-8 with tuned-port injection was genuinely available, but it lost twenty-five horsepower (from 215-horsepower to 190) due to camshaft changes.

All the car magazines talked about Corvette 350-cid engines in 1986 Camaros, and several magazines actually tested prototypes. But last minute glitches prevented any of the bigger motors from being sold to the public during Camaro's 1986 model year.

One of eight announced new colors for 1986, Light Brown (Code #60) was dropped from the dealer order guides before production officially began, but Chevrolet records show four were built.

Aftermarket companies sold rear window louver kits for third-generation Camaros almost as soon as 1982 models debuted; in 1986, Chevrolet offered its

Yes, the Berlinetta model was available in 1986, but only for the first few months of production. Despite (or perhaps because of) its fancy electronic instrumentation, sales of the "Luxury" Camaro never reached the levels Chevrolet had hoped for. Sales in 1986 were just 4,479. Chevrolet photo.

own. It was RPO DE1 at $210.00. Despite a late introduction, 6,058 were sold in 1986 Camaros.

The good news for 1987 was the return of a convertible to the Camaro stable, the first since 1969. The bad news was it cost a little more. In 1969, convertible Camaros were built on Chevrolet's production lines with the coupes. Then, a V-8 convertible Camaro set you back all of $213 more than the coupe. In 1987 Chevrolet shipped completed coupes to another company, ASC (Automobile Specialty Company) for the convertible conversion. In the Z28, this convert-conversion jolted you to the tune of a $17,632 base price, $4,399 more than a Z28 coupe.

A Type LT model Camaro was available from 1973 through 1978, so Chevrolet revived the LT name for the 1987 Camaro as something of a replacement for the departed Berlinetta, but the fancy instrument panel died with the Berlinetta

Although an option rather than a separate model, the LT Camaro at top was new for 1987 and plugged the gap left by the discontinued Berlinetta. But the big Camaro story for 1987 was the return of a convertible for the first time since 1969. The photo shows the IROC-Z version, but the Sport Coupe, LT Sport Coupe and Z28 models could all be ordered as convertibles. Chevrolet photos.

name. And the earlier Type LT and Berlinetta Camaros were separate models. For 1987, the LT was an option to be added to Sport Coupes or Sport Coupe Convertibles, just as the IROC was an option for Z28 models. To *simplify* ordering 1987 Camaros, Chevrolet started bundling options into packages. There were three or four packages for each Camaro Sport Coupe, Sport Coupe Convertible, Z28 Coupe, Z28 Convertible, and for each of the LT and IROC variants. This added up to twenty-eight option packages, each of which had from three to six

1987 Camaro Colors/Options

Color Code	Body Color
13	Silver
23	Bright Blue
28	Dark Blue
40	White
41	Black
51	Yellow
68	Dark Brown
74	Dark Red
81	Bright Red
87	Medium Gray

INTERIOR COLORS: Black, Gray, Red, Saddle

Order #	Item Description	Sticker $
1FP87	Camaro Sport Coupe	10,409.00
1FP87	Camaro Sport Coupe Convertible	15,208.00
1FP87	Z28 Camaro Sport Coupe	13,233.00
1FP87	Z28 Camaro Sport Coupe Convertible	17,632.00
B4E	Base LT Group (w/Sp Cpe)	1,522.00
B4E	Base LT Group (w/conv)	1,358.00
B4Z	Base IROC Group (w/Z28)	669.00
B4Z	Base IROC Group (w/Z28 conv)	699.00
AM9	Seat Back, Split Folding Rear	50.00
AU3	Door Lock System, Power	145.00
A01	Glass, Tinted	120.00
B2L	Engine, 225-hp, 350-cid V-8 (w/IROC)	1,045.00
B48	Luggage Compt Trim (w/Sp Cpe)	164.00
B48	Luggage Compt Trim (w/Z28)	84.00
B84	Moldings, Body Side	60.00
B91	Moldings, Door Edge, Black	15.00
CC1	Roof Panels, Removable Glass	866.00
C49	Defogger, Rear Window Electric	145.00
C60	Air Conditioning	775.00
DE1	Louvers, Rear Window	210.00
G80	Axle, Limited Slip	100.00
G92	Axle, Performance Ratio (w/IROC Z28)	21.00
J65	Brakes, Power Disc Front and Rear	179.00
KC4	Cooler, Engine Oil (w/IROC Z28)	110.00
LB9	Engine, 190-hp, 305-cid V8 (w/Z28)	745.00
LG4	Engine, 165-hp, 305-cid V-8 (w/Sp Cpe)	400.00
MM5	Transmission, 5-speed	n/c
MX0	Transmission, Automatic	490.00
PE1	Wheels, Cast Aluminum (w/LT)	215.00
QDX	Tires, P195/70R-14 BW (w/LT)	90.00
QDZ	Tires, P245/60R-15 BW (w/IROC)	n/c
QHX	Tires, P205/70R-14 BW (w/LT)	n/c
QHY	Tires, P205/70R-14 WW (w/LT)	76.00
QYH	Tires, P215/65R-15 Ltr (w/Sp Cpe)	102.00
QYZ	Tires, P215/65R-15 BW (w/Z28)	-102.00

Order #	Item Description	Sticker $
UA1	Battery, Heavy-Duty	26.00
UL5	Radio Delete	*
UL6	Radio, AM, Clock	*
UM6	AM-FM St, Cass, SS, Clk	*
UM7	AM St, FM St, Cass, SS, Clk	*
UU8	Delco-Bose Stereo System	*
UX1	AM St, FM St, Cass, SS, Clk, EQ	*
U75	Antenna, Power	70.00
C—2	Cloth Seats (w/Sp Cpe & Z28)	28.00
F—2	Custom Cloth Seats (w/Sp Cpe & Z28)	277.00
A—2	Leather Seats (w/LT)	473.00
A—2	Leather Seats (w/Sp Cpe & Z28)	750.00
1SA	Sport Coupe Option Package 1	n/c
1SB	Sport Coupe Option Package 2	1,212.00
1SC	Sport Coupe Option Package 3	1,628.00
1SD	Sport Coupe Option Package 4	2,126.00
1SA	LT Option Package 1	1,522.00
1SB	LT Option Package 2	1,938.00
1SC	LT Option Package 3	2,387.00
1SD	LT Option Package 4	2,858.00
1SA	Z28 Option Package 1	n/c
1SB	Z28 Option Package 2	1,999.00
1SC	Z28 Option Package 3 (w/o cargo cover)	2,470.00
1SD	Z28 Option Package 3 (w/cargo cover)	2,539.00
1SA	IROC Option Package 1	669.00
1SB	IROC Option Package 2	2,409.00
1SC	IROC Option Package 3 (w/o cargo cover)	3,204.00
1SC	IROC Option Package 3 (w/cargo cover)	3,273.00
1SA	Sp Cpe Conv Option Package 1	n/c
1SB	Sp Cpe Conv Option Package 2	1,212.00
1SC	Sp Cpe Conv Option Package 3	1,559.00
1SD	Sp Cpe Conv Option Package 4	1,889.00
1SA	LT Conv Option Package 1	1,358.00
1SB	LT Conv Option Package 2	1,705.00
1SC	LT Conv Option Package 3	2,035.00
1SD	LT Conv Option Package 4	2,376.00
1SA	Z28 Conv Option Package 1	n/c
1SB	Z28 Conv. Option Package 2	1,900.00
1SC	Z28 Conv Option Package 3	2,241.00
1SA	IROC Conv Option Package 1	699.00
1SB	IROC Conv Option Package 2	2,359.00
1SC	IROC Conv Option Package 3	2,975.00

- Prices shown were introductory retail.
- Most options shown were available individually, but some of these and others not available individually were grouped in different option packages.

*Radio prices varied depending on option package.

radio choices, all differently priced. Some options, like cruise control, tilt steering and power seat, weren't available individually so astute customers accustomed to ordering exactly what they wanted could no longer do so.

As for engines, the four-cylinder was gone for sure; the RPO LB8 V-6 was the base powerplant. The RPO L69 High Output optional engine was also dropped, but the 350-cid "Corvette" engine came aboard. This RPO BL2 had 225-horsepower, a price of $1,045, and could only be specified with IROC Z28 models. Everyone liked to call this the Corvette engine, but there were differences. The Camaro version had iron cylinder heads instead of aluminum, iron exhaust manifolds instead of stainless steel, and it delivered fifteen less horsepower.

New options were highlighted by genuine leather seat trim and a Delco-Bose (RPO UU8) sound system.

Chevrolet increased its extended warranty coverage for Camaros in March 1987, retroactive for all 1987 Camaro models.

There's no arguing that third-generation Camaros were beautifully styled with handling and performance to match. But what about reliability? Generally, the record has been excellent. But nobody's perfect. Here are some third-generation problem areas that have been passed on to me by Chevrolet dealer service managers and mechanics.

The lift-off roof panels had leak problems until a new sealing material was introduced into production in March 1984. The new sealing material can be retrofitted into earlier-production third-generation cars and it has proven to be an effective fix. Fortunately, when the panels leaked, the water usually ran down the side door glass and into the door itself, then out the door drain holes. Upholstery was seldom damaged.

Third-generation Camaro owners have complained about minor hesitation and sluggish throttle response with the throttle-body-injected V-8's, but V-8's with four-barrel carburetion have also been singled out for apparent fuel starvation under hard acceleration. Chevrolet determined the likely cause to be vapor lock, and issued dealer repair kits for both the RPO L69 and RPO LG4 V-8's consisting of new fuel pumps and other hardware.

Differential noise in third-generation Camaros was cured when Chevrolet revised the torque-assembly specs. Growling from a Positraction unit could also be simple neglect. Posi units should have their fluid changed, including new additive, about every 15,000 miles. But even when an owner has neglected a Positraction unit, it can usually be cured with the new fluid/additive treatment.

The wide Eagle GT tires (Goodyear) used on Z-28's had a tendency to wear at the edges, especially if not rotated at prescribed intervals, or if pressures weren't carefully watched. These tires are expensive to replace, so when looking at a third-generation Camaro so equipped, check them.

Though it followed Ford's Mustang into the marketplace, the Camaro has set the pace since, always remaining true to its mission. It is America's affordable enthusiast car. It's the car the other would-be providers aim their sights on.

The baseball, hot dogs, apple pie folks at Chevrolet hope to keep it that way.

CAMARO PRICES

Source: *The Gold Book*

Newer Camaros are in the depreciation cycle and their values change monthly. Auto dealers subscribe to one or more used-car value guides published at frequent intervals. The prices in these guides are determined by sampling selling prices reported by dealers throughout the country. Most used cars sold by dealers are eight years old or less, so the dealer guides concentrate on those.

It's more difficult to determine the value of older Camaros, but the best guide I know of is *The Gold Book.* It lists values for most 1955 through 1980 model automobiles and trucks. The editor, Quentin Craft, has been in the auto business since 1935. His experience, along with prices gleaned from collector auctions around the country, make *The Gold Book* a useful tool to combine with your own evaluation of condition, options, and documentation.

The prices below are reprinted here with permission of Quentin Craft and are from the second quarter, 1987 edition. Subscription cost for one year (four issues) is $36. Write *The Gold Book*, 1462 Vanderbilt, El Paso, TX 79935-9990.

	Fair	Good	Excel
1967			
6-Cyl Coupe	3,170	4,875	7,500
6-Cyl Conv	4,225	6,500	10,000
SS396 Coupe	3,380	5,200	8,000
Z28 Coupe	4,650	7,150	11,000
Pace Car	5,280	8,125	12,500
•Add 1,000 for V-8, SS, Rally Sport			
1968			
6-Cyl Coupe	2,325	3,575	5,500
6-Cyl Conv	2,745	4,225	6,500
8-Cyl Coupe	3,170	4,875	7,500
8-Cyl Conv	4,225	6,500	10,000
•Add 1,800 for Z28			
1969			
6-Cyl Coupe	2,115	3,250	5,000
6-Cyl Conv	2,325	3,575	5,500
8-Cyl Coupe	3,170	4,875	7,500
8-Cyl Conv	4,650	7,150	11,000
•Add 1,700 for Z28, 500 for SS396			
1970			
2-Dr Coupe	2,960	4,550	7,000
•Add $800 for SS396			

	Fair	Good	Excel
1971			
2-Dr Coupe	1,480	2,275	3,500
Z28 Coupe	2,325	3,575	5,500
1972			
6-Cyl Coupe	1,055	1,625	2,500
8-Cyl Coupe	1,480	2,275	3,500
•Add 700 for Z28			
1973			
8-Cyl Coupe	1,365	2,100	3,000
SS Coupe	1,820	2,800	4,000
•Add 1,000 for Z28			
1974			
8-Cyl Coupe	1,455	2,240	3,200
Z28 Coupe	1,730	2,660	3,800
•Deduct 400 for 6-Cyl			
1975			
8-Cyl Coupe	1,275	1,820	2,600
•Deduct 400 for 6-Cyl			

	Fair	Good	Excel
1976			
8-Cyl Coupe	1,315	1,875	2,500
•Deduct 350 for 6-Cyl			
1977			
Z28 Coupe	1,890	2,700	3,600
Type LT	1,785	2,550	3,400
6-Cyl Coupe	1,470	2,100	2,800
1978			
Rally 6-Cyl	1,845	2,525	3,280
LT 6-Cyl	1,805	2,470	3,210
Rally Z28	2,305	3,155	4,100
V-8 Coupe	1,935	2,650	3,440
1979			
Rally 6-Cyl	2,090	2,715	3,480
Sport Coupe	2,005	2,605	3,340
Berlinetta	2,050	2,660	3,410
Z28 Coupe	2,705	3,510	4,500

RECOMMENDED CAMARO BOOKS

Camaro books available to the enthusiast range from brief reprints of factory data sheets to meticulously researched, hardbound historicals. Each has something to offer; here are five I can recommend without hesitation.

Antonick, M. B. *The Camaro White Book.* Powell, Ohio: Michael Bruce Associates, Inc., 1985.

Dobbins, M. F. and Incremona, F. J. R. *Camaro 1967-1969 Fact Book.* Glenside, Pennsylvania: Dr. M. F. Dobbins, 1984.

Lamm, Michael. *Camaro: The Third Generation.* Stockton, California: Lamm-Morada Publishing Company, Inc., 1981.

———*The Camaro Book From A Through Z-28.* Stockton, California: Lamm-Morada Publishing Company, Inc., 1981, 1984.

Witzenburg, Gary L. *Camaro! From Challenger to Champion: The Complete Camaro History.* Princeton, New Jersey: Princeton Publishing Company, 1981.

MORE GREAT READING

Illustrated Ferrari Buyer's Guide. Features all street/production cars 1954 through 1980. 176 pages, over 225 photos, softbound.

Illustrated Porsche Buyer's Guide. Covers the 356 through the 944 from 1950 to 1983 with lots of photos. Softbound, 175 pages.

Illustrated Corvette Buyer's Guide. Includes 194 photos and lots of info on all these cars 1953-1982. 156 pages, softbound.

Illustrated High Performance Mustang Buyer's Guide. Covers the 1965 GT, the Shelby, through the 1973 Mach 1. Softbound, 250 illustrations, 176 pages.

Illustrated Alfa Romeo Buyer's Guide. The 6C-2500 through the Montreal are covered with over 200 illustrations. 176 pages, softbound.

Illustrated M.G. Buyer's Guide. Features all the models 1924 through 1982. 160 pages, softbound, over 125 illustrations.

Illustrated Lamborghini Buyer's Guide. Details all models from the first V-12-engined 350 GTV through the 1983 LMA models including many specials. 176 pages, over 250 photos, softbound.

Illustrated Austin-Healey Buyer's Guide. The 100 through the 300 through the Jensen-Healey are covered with over 125 great illustrations. Softbound, 136 pages.

Illustrated Rolls-Royce, Bentley Buyer's Guide. Covers prewar 1907 Silver Ghost through present models including the Silver Spirit and Mulsanne. 176 pages, over 150 illustrations, softbound.

Illustrated BMW Buyer's Guide. From the early 500 through the 7-Series and the M1. 176 pages, softbound, over 175 illustrations.

Illustrated Jaguar Buyer's Guide. Includes over 160 illustrations of the SS 100 through the elegant sedans of the eighties. 156 pages, softbound.

Illustrated Maserati Buyer's Guide. Covers all models up through the Biturbo. 136 pages over 120 illustrations, softbound.

Illustrated Triumph Buyer's Guide. Features models from TR1 through TR8 including Spitfire, GT6, Stag and more. Nearly 200 illustrations, 176 pages, softbound.

The Big Healeys: A Collector's Guide, by Graham Robson. 128 pages, 130 illustrations.

Classic Jaguar Saloons: A Collector's Guide, by Chris Harvey. 128 pages, 135 illustrations.

The Jaguar E-Type: A Collector's Guide, by Paul Skilleter. 128 pages, 160 illustrations.

The Jaguar XK: A Collector's Guide, by Paul Skilleter. 128 pages, 140 illustrations.

The Lotus Elan and Europa: A Collector's Guide, by John Bolster. 126 pages, 135 illustrations.

MG: The Art of Abingdon, by John McLellan. Lavish pictorial history of Britain's famous sports car and its factory. 256 pages, 480 illustrations.

The MGA, MGB & MGC: A Collector's Guide, by Graham Robson. 136 pages, 146 illustrations.

The Porsche 911: A Collector's Guide, by Michael Cotton. 128 pages, 140 illustrations.

The Sprites & Midgets: A Collector's Guide, by Eric Dymock. 128 pages, 130 illustrations.

The T-Series MG: A Collector's Guide, by Graham Robson. 128 pages, 131 illustrations.

The Triumph TRs: A Collector's Guide, by Graham Robson. 150 pages, 200 illustrations.

The Z-Series Datsuns: A Collector's Guide, by Ray Hutton. 128 pages, 140 illustrations.

The Story of Lotus: 1947–1960, Birth of a Legend, By Ian H. Smith. 192 pages, 180 illustrations.

The Story of Lotus: 1961–1971, Growth of a Legend, by Doug Nye. 288 pages, 280 illustrations.

Triumph Cars: The Complete 75-Year History, by Richard Langworth and Graham Robson. Over 400 pictures supplement this definitive history along with comprehensive appendices. 312 pages.

The Corvettes 1953–1984: A Collector's Guide, by Richard Langworth. 128 pages, 130 illustrations.

Lamborghini: A Collector's Guide, by Chris Harvey. 128 pages, 127 illustrations.

Motorbooks International
Publishers & Wholesalers Inc.
Osceola, Wisconsin 54020, USA ®